Great American
Journeys

EXPLORE AMERICA

Great American Journeys

Reader's Digest

THE READER'S DIGEST ASSOCIATION, INC.
Pleasantville, New York / Montreal

GREAT AMERICAN JOURNEYS was created and produced by St. Remy Press.

STAFF FOR GREAT AMERICAN JOURNEYS
Series Editor: Elizabeth Cameron
Art Director: Chantal Bilodeau
Editor: Alfred LeMaitre
Photo Researcher: Geneviève Monette
Cartography: Hélène Dion, Anne-Marie Lemay, David Widgington
Researchers: Jennifer Meltzer, Robert B. Ronald
Contributing Researcher: Joan McKenna
Index: Christine Jacobs
System Coordinator: Éric Beaulieu
Technical Support: Mathieu Raymond-Beaubien
Scanner Operators: Martin Francoeur, Sara Grynspan

ST. REMY STAFF
PUBLISHER: Kenneth Winchester
PRESIDENT, CHIEF EXECUTIVE OFFICER: Fernand Lecoq
PRESIDENT, CHIEF OPERATING OFFICER: Pierre Léveillé
VICE PRESIDENT, FINANCE: Natalie Watanabe
MANAGING EDITOR: Carolyn Jackson
MANAGING ART DIRECTOR: Diane Denoncourt
PRODUCTION MANAGER: Michelle Turbide

Writers: Rita Aryoshi—The Royal Route
Bob Devine—The Coast Starlight,
Durango & Silverton Narrow Gauge Railroad
David Dunbar—The Hudson River
Kim Heacox—The Inside Passage
Jim Henderson—Mark Twain's River
Rose Houk—Rafting the Colorado River
Jonathan Nicholas—The Oregon Trail
M. Timothy O'Keefe—The Overseas Highway
James S. Wamsley—The Blue Ridge Parkway

Contributing Writers: Adriana Barton,
Pierre Home-Douglas, Elizabeth W. Lewis,
Nancy Lyon, Gerry Shikatani

READER'S DIGEST STAFF
Series Editor: Gayla Visali
Editor: Jill Maynard
Art Director: Evelyn Bauer
Art Editor: Nancy Mace

READER'S DIGEST GENERAL BOOKS
Editor-in-Chief, Books and Home Entertainment:
Barbara J. Morgan
Editor, U.S. General Books: Susan Wernert Lewis
Editorial Director: Jane Polley
Art Director: Evelyn Bauer
Research Director: Laurel A. Gilbride
Affinity Directors: Will Bradbury, Jim Dwyer, Joseph Gonzalez, Kaari Ward
Design Directors: Perri DeFino, Robert M. Grant, Joel Musler
Business Manager: Vidya Tejwani
Copy Chief: Edward W. Atkinson
Picture Editor: Marion Bodine
Head Librarian: Jo Manning

READER'S DIGEST PRODUCTION
Assistant Production Supervisor: Mike Gallo
Prepress Specialist: Karen Goldsmith
Quality Control Manager: Ann Kennedy Harris
Assistant Production Manager: Michael R. Kuzma

Book Production Director: Ken Gillett
Prepress Manager: Gary Hansen
Book Production Manager: Patricia M. Heinz
U.S. Prepress Manager: Mark P. Merritt

Library of Congress Cataloging in Publication Data

Great American journeys.
        p.   cm.—(Explore America)
     Includes index.
     ISBN 0-89577-847-5
     1. United States—Guidebooks.   I. Reader's Digest Association.
     II. Series
     E158.G83   1996
     917.304'929—dc20   95-24913

Opening photographs
Cover: Durango & Silverton Narrow Gauge Railroad, Colorado
Back Cover: St. Francis of Assisi Church, Taos, New Mexico
Page 2: Tidal marsh along the Hudson River, New York
Page 5: South Cascade Mountains at sunset, Washington

CONTENTS

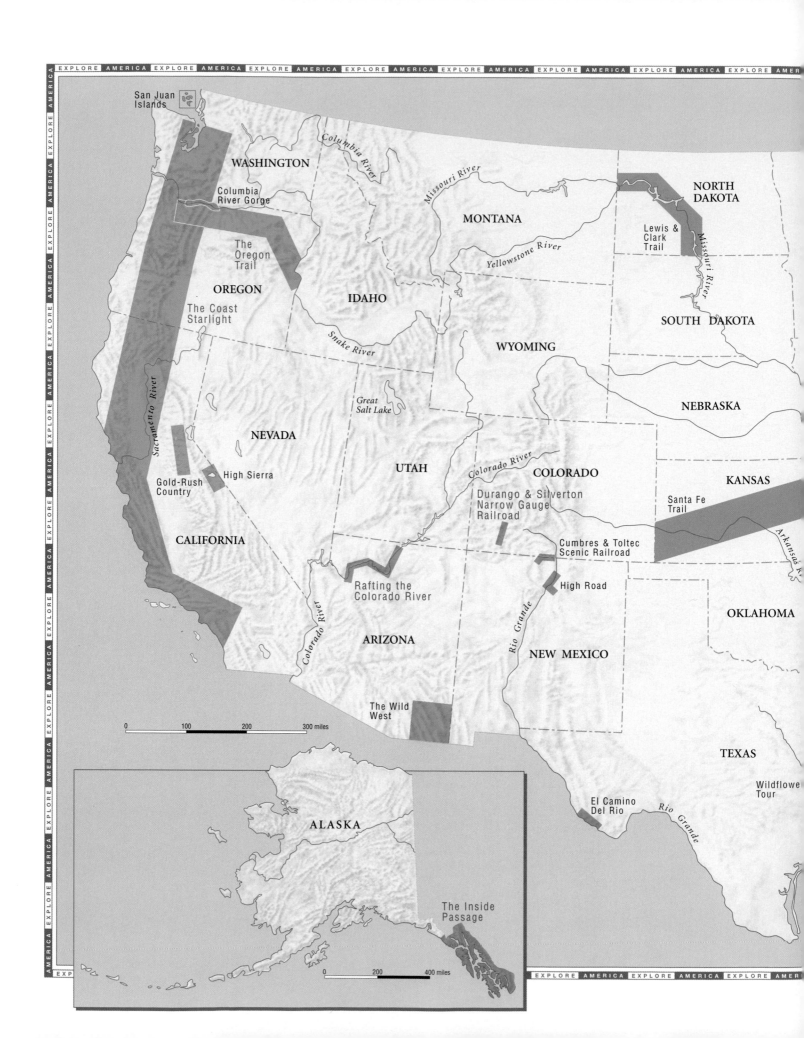

San Juan
Islands

Columbia River

WASHINGTON

Columbia
River Gorge

MONTANA

Missouri River

NORTH
DAKOTA

Lewis &
Clark
Trail

Missouri River

The
Oregon
Trail

Yellowstone River

OREGON

IDAHO

The Coast
Starlight

Snake River

SOUTH DAKOTA

WYOMING

Sacramento River

Great
Salt Lake

NEVADA

Gold-Rush
Country

High Sierra

UTAH

NEBRASKA

Colorado River

COLORADO

Durango & Silverton
Narrow Gauge
Railroad

KANSAS

Santa Fe
Trail

Arkansas R.

CALIFORNIA

Cumbres & Toltec
Scenic Railroad

Rafting the
Colorado River

High Road

OKLAHOMA

Colorado River

ARIZONA

Rio Grande

NEW MEXICO

The Wild
West

TEXAS

Wildflower
Tour

El Camino
Del Rio

Rio Grande

0   100   200   300 miles

ALASKA

The Inside
Passage

0   200   400 miles

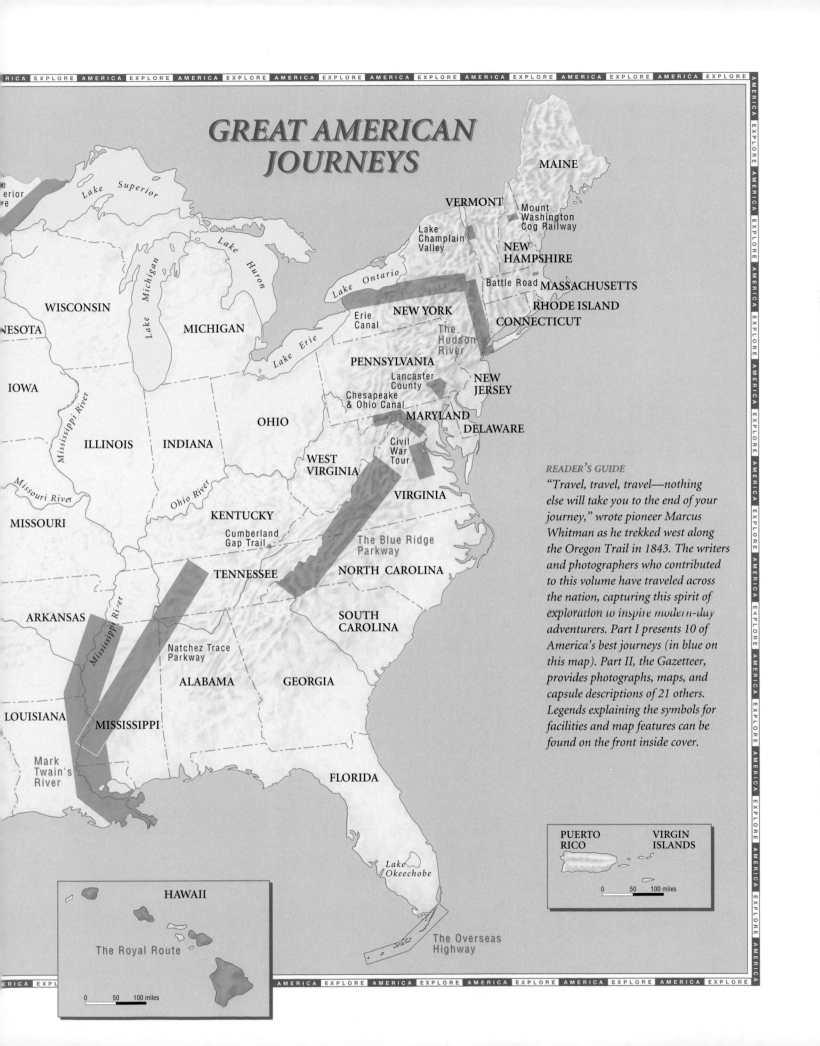

GREAT AMERICAN JOURNEYS

MAINE

VERMONT

Mount
Washington
Cog Railway

Lake
Champlain
Valley

NEW
HAMPSHIRE

Lake Superior

Lake Superior

erior
ve

Lake Ontario

Battle Road MASSACHUSETTS

WISCONSIN

Lake Michigan

Lake Huron

MICHIGAN

Erie
Canal

NEW YORK

RHODE ISLAND

CONNECTICUT

NESOTA

IOWA

Lake Erie

The
Hudson
River

PENNSYLVANIA

Mississippi River

Lancaster
County

NEW
JERSEY

Chesapeake
& Ohio Canal

OHIO

MARYLAND

ILLINOIS

INDIANA

DELAWARE

Missouri River

Civil
War
Tour

WEST
VIRGINIA

VIRGINIA

Ohio River

MISSOURI

KENTUCKY

Cumberland
Gap Trail

The Blue Ridge
Parkway

TENNESSEE

NORTH CAROLINA

ARKANSAS

Mississippi River

SOUTH
CAROLINA

Natchez Trace
Parkway

ALABAMA

GEORGIA

LOUISIANA

MISSISSIPPI

Mark
Twain's
River

FLORIDA

Lake
Okeechobe

READER'S GUIDE

*"Travel, travel, travel—nothing
else will take you to the end of your
journey," wrote pioneer Marcus
Whitman as he trekked west along
the Oregon Trail in 1843. The writers
and photographers who contributed
to this volume have traveled across
the nation, capturing this spirit of
exploration to inspire modern-day
adventurers. Part I presents 10 of
America's best journeys (in blue on
this map). Part II, the Gazetteer,
provides photographs, maps, and
capsule descriptions of 21 others.
Legends explaining the symbols for
facilities and map features can be
found on the front inside cover.*

PUERTO
RICO

VIRGIN
ISLANDS

0   50   100 miles

HAWAII

The Royal Route

0   50   100 miles

The Overseas
Highway

THE HUDSON RIVER

*New York's historic river unites
matchless scenery and some of
the nation's grandest homes.*

When English explorer Henry Hudson
sailed his 80-ton *Half Moon* up the Great
River of the Mountains in 1609 to what is now
Albany, he met with disappointment: the great
river that today bears his name did not lead to
the Orient, as he had hoped, so Hudson returned
home. Although the river's 315-mile length places
it only 71st among America's longest rivers, the
Hudson became the stage on which the drama
of America's early history was played.

There are many ways to approach the pageant
of the river, from its many-storied past to its fascinating present. Most visitors journey along the
network of highways that snakes down the
Hudson Valley. Others opt for the unfolding
panorama of the railroad, which follows a waterline route that offers unforgettable river vistas.
Several companies offer river cruises that allow
visitors to savor the Hudson as its discoverer
might have done.

The first Europeans to settle in the region were
the Dutch, who established estates, towns, and

SHORELINE BLUFFS
A paved walking and cycling trail runs alongside the river in Beach State Park, located in Nyack. The park's spectacular scenery beckons visitors to stop awhile and admire the river and the wooded bluffs that rise along its shoreline.

BRIDGING THE RIVER
Overleaf: Framed by fall foliage, the dramatic Bear Mountain Bridge spans the Hudson near Peekskill. The 1,632-foot-long bridge is one of five between Albany and Tarrytown. Bear Mountain State Park, on the river's western bank, is a popular getaway spot for New Yorkers.

churches along the length of the river during the early 1600's. Throughout the Revolutionary War, the Hudson's strategic location made it a hotly contested battleground. In more peaceful times, however, the river has inspired numerous writers, as well as the nation's first homegrown group of painters—the Hudson River School. In the mid-1800's, artists such as Thomas Cole, Asher B. Durand, Frederick Church, and Albert Bierstadt captured on canvas poetic landscapes of forested slopes, shimmering waters, idyllic farms and vineyards, shad fishermen, and craggy gorges.

The Hudson River played a pivotal role in the development of American commerce and industry, acting as a highway for goods and people moving into the interior. Today visitors can follow the same route taken by the Indians, explorers, steamboat pilots, fur traders, pioneers, canal builders, railroad men, and soldiers who came before them.

PATH TO THE SEA

The source of the Hudson is a two-acre pond, romantically named Lake Tear of the Clouds, on the southwestern slope of Mount Marcy in the Adirondacks, south of Lake Placid. From its humble beginnings, the river rushes crystal-clear through Adirondack forests of beech, birch, and maple trees, churning over rapids and gliding into deep pools. South of the Adirondack foothills, locks and dams tame the Hudson into a 40-mile-long chain of sluggish lakes flanked by pastures and melon fields. South of Troy, where a dam impounds the waterway for the last time, the Hudson receives the flow of its principal tributary, the Mohawk River.

INFORMATION FOR VISITORS

Hwy. 87 (New York State Thruway) runs along the western side of the Hudson River from Albany to New York City. Hwy. 9 roughly parallels it on the eastern side. Bridges across the Hudson are toll. Regular Amtrak train service from Pennsylvania Station stops at Croton-on-Hudson, Poughkeepsie, Rhinecliff, Hudson, and Albany. Several companies offer daily boat tours from May through November. New York Waterways operates round-trips from Manhattan to Tarrytown and "Hudson Highland" cruises from West Point to Newburgh. The National Park Service maintains the Franklin Delano Roosevelt National Historic Site, together with the Eleanor Roosevelt Center at Val-Kill and the Vanderbilt Mansion National Historic Site. The New York State Office of Parks, Recreation, and Historic Preservation maintains the Mills Mansion at Staatsburg, Clermont on the Hudson, and Frederic E. Church's house at Olana. Some sites are open for only part of the year. For more information: Hudson Valley Tourism, P.O. Box 284, Salt Point, NY 12578; (800) 232-4782.

FOREST FLORA
The forests that cloak the rounded hills of the Hudson Valley contain more than a dozen species of oak trees, and shelter a diverse plant life that includes wild geraniums, above.

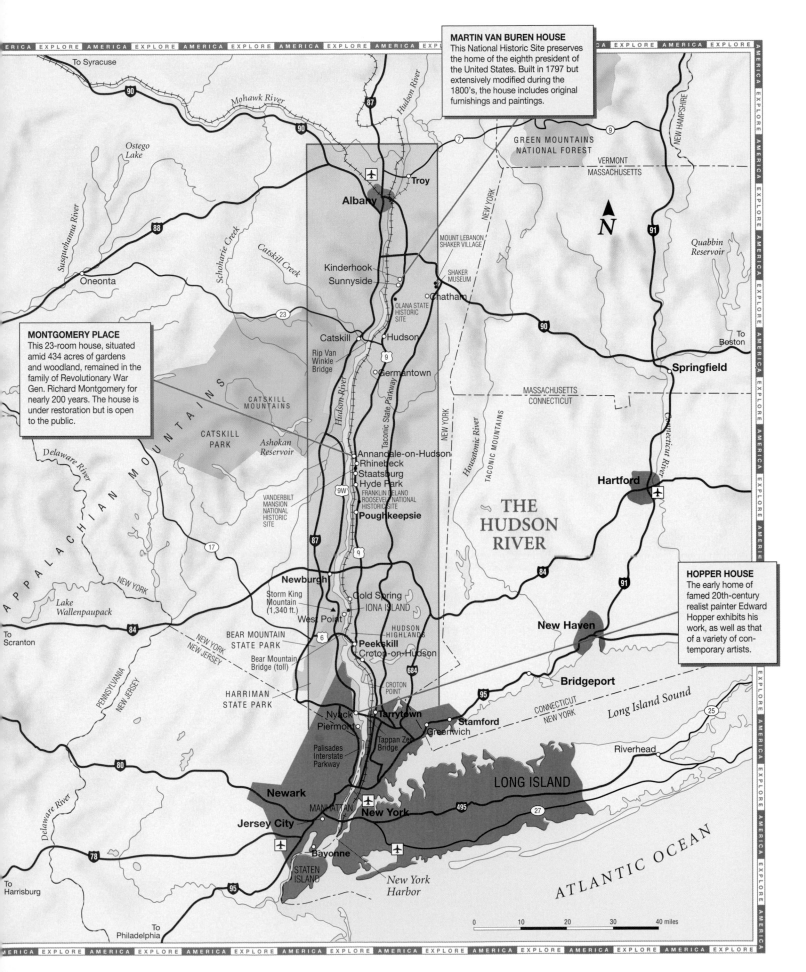

MARTIN VAN BUREN HOUSE
This National Historic Site preserves the home of the eighth president of the United States. Built in 1797 but extensively modified during the 1800's, the house includes original furnishings and paintings.

MONTGOMERY PLACE
This 23-room house, situated amid 434 acres of gardens and woodland, remained in the family of Revolutionary War Gen. Richard Montgomery for nearly 200 years. The house is under restoration but is open to the public.

HOPPER HOUSE
The early home of famed 20th-century realist painter Edward Hopper exhibits his work, as well as that of a variety of contemporary artists.

To Syracuse

Mohawk River

Hudson River

90

87

7

9

GREEN MOUNTAINS
NATIONAL FOREST

NEW HAMPSHIRE

VERMONT
MASSACHUSETTS

Ostego Lake

Troy

Albany

91

Quabbin Reservoir

88

Schoharie Creek

Catskill Creek

MOUNT LEBANON
SHAKER VILLAGE

Kinderhook

Sunnyside

SHAKER MUSEUM

Chatham

Oneonta

90

To Boston

23

Catskill

Hudson

9

Springfield

Susquehanna River

Rip Van Winkle Bridge

Germantown

MASSACHUSETTS
CONNECTICUT

CATSKILL
MOUNTAINS

Taconic State Parkway

NEW YORK

CATSKILL
PARK

Ashokan Reservoir

Housatonic River

TACONIC MOUNTAINS

Delaware River

Annandale-on-Hudson
Rhinebeck
Staatsburg
Hyde Park

Hartford

9W

VANDERBILT
MANSION
NATIONAL
HISTORIC
SITE

FRANKLIN DELANO
ROOSEVELT NATIONAL
HISTORIC SITE

THE
HUDSON
RIVER

Poughkeepsie

Connecticut River

17

NEW YORK

84

91

87

9

Lake Wallenpaupack

Newburgh

Storm King Mountain (1,340 ft.)

Cold Spring
IONA ISLAND

West Point

HUDSON
HIGHLANDS

New Haven

To Scranton

84

BEAR MOUNTAIN
STATE PARK

6

Peekskill
Croton-on-Hudson

684

Bridgeport

NEW YORK
NEW JERSEY

Bear Mountain Bridge (toll)

CROTON
POINT

95

CONNECTICUT
NEW YORK

Long Island Sound

25

PENNSYLVANIA

NEW JERSEY

HARRIMAN
STATE PARK

Nyack
Piermont

Tarrytown

Stamford
Greenwich

Riverhead

80

Tappan Zee Bridge

Palisades
Interstate
Parkway

LONG ISLAND

Newark

Delaware River

MANHATTAN

New York

495

27

Jersey City

78

Bayonne

STATEN
ISLAND

New York Harbor

ATLANTIC OCEAN

95

To Harrisburg

To Philadelphia

0   10   20   30   40 miles

MARSHY REFUGE
Sailors regard Iona Island, where tidal marshes shelter extensive bird life, as the point where the sea breeze ceases.

From here south to Battery Park, on Manhattan's southern tip, is the Hudson River's heartland. This lower portion of the river is actually an estuary—an arm of the sea gouged out by glaciers—deep enough for navigation by oceangoing vessels. Because this section of the river is at sea level, high tide pulses twice daily all the way up to Troy, 150 miles from the Atlantic.

In the 70 miles from Albany to Newburgh, the nearly currentless river eases past sandbars, islands, and marshes amid countryside largely unspoiled by development. To the west the purpled mass of the Catskill Mountains looms like dark clouds along the horizon. To the east lie the lower, rounded hills of Connecticut's Taconic Mountains.

South of Newburgh the river narrows and enters its most dramatic stretch, the Hudson Highlands— the only place where the Appalachian Mountains are breached by a river at sea level. Many people consider the Highlands to be the most beautiful stretch of river in America. The northern gateway to this 15-mile gorge is guarded by 1,340-foot Storm King Mountain, a dome of ancient granite

rising steeply from the riverbank. Other brooding, heavily forested mountains crowd both shores, much as they did in Henry Hudson's day. Released from its Highland corset below Peekskill, the Hudson swells to three miles wide at Haverstraw Bay. The nine-mile reach between Croton Point and Piermont Marsh was wide enough for the Dutch to call it Tappan Zee (*zee* means "sea").

South of this broad expanse, the river narrows between Manhattan Island and the Palisades. For about 60 million years the Hudson actually flowed west of this sheer rock wall to empty into the ocean south of Staten Island. The rampart, which extends 50 miles between 827-foot Mount Tor and Staten Island, was formed about 200 million years ago when tremendous flows of magma solidified between layers of sandstone and shale, hardening into a rock called diabase that was tough enough to withstand eons of erosion. About 15 million years ago the river found a more direct route to the sea. Thereafter, the Hudson flowed east of the Palisades to the Atlantic. New Jersey preserves 12 miles of this columnar basalt cliff, which the Indians called Weehawken, or "rows of trees."

Beginning about 1 million years ago, four great continental glaciers ground south in succession, each one gouging the Hudson riverbed deeper. As the ice melted some 15,000 years ago at the close of the final phase of glaciation, sea levels rose and the Atlantic Ocean began to flow up the Hudson, "drowning" it. When Algonquian Indians discovered the tidal river, it fulfilled a prophecy that said that they would live "by water that flows two ways."

A VALLEY TOUR

Between Albany and New York, the Hudson offers up its treasures, both past and present. At the state capital in Albany, government buildings stand on the site of Fort Orange, a Dutch post established in 1624 as the northern limit of their New World colony.

South of Albany, the Hudson stitches together a collection of quaint towns, historic landmarks, and an eclectic assemblage of museums. A short drive east of the river near the village of Old Chatham is the Shaker Museum, housing one of the nation's finest collections of Shaker furniture. Eight buildings were moved here to display the museum's exhibits, which, in addition to traditionally styled furniture, feature oval boxes, woven baskets, furniture, tools, and machinery. Displays

TAPPAN ZEE TWILIGHT
Tarrytown's sweeping views of the Hudson, shown above as dusk colors the western sky and the Tappan Zee Bridge, made it a fashionable retreat during the 1870's.

PUMPKIN ROW
In the fall, roadside stalls give visitors the opportunity to sample the region's natural bounty, which includes pumpkins, blueberries, apples, and squash. Many farms offer visitors the chance to pick their own fresh produce.

include a working blacksmith and cabinet-making and weaving shops. Mount Lebanon Shaker Village, located a few miles away, was once the spiritual center of the sect.

The port town of Hudson, settled by whalers and merchant families from New England after the Revolution, is the home of the American Museum of Firefighting. This unique museum boasts the oldest and most comprehensive collection of firefighting equipment and memorabilia in the nation, some dating back to 1725. At the Old Rhinebeck Aerodrome, just outside the elegant resort town of Rhinebeck, the early history of aviation takes to the skies in the form of a world-famous collection of vintage airplanes. Mock dogfights by World War I fighters are a part of regular weekend airshows. Visitors can even inspect the Hudson Valley aboard a 1929 New Standard D-25 open biplane.

To encourage settlement of the Hudson Valley between New Amsterdam (New York) and Fort Orange, the Dutch West India Company granted large tracts of land to *patroons*—entrepreneurs who had to colonize their land holdings with at least 50 people within four years. The English, who took over the colony in 1664 and renamed it New York, also established substantial estates along the river. Rather than spur agricultural development, these large and economically unsound estates left the Hudson lightly settled for two centuries, ensuring that much of the land remained undeveloped.

Latter-day patroons, such as Robert Livingston, Frederick Vanderbilt, and Jay Gould, built their residences along the river's east bank. Today many of these sumptuous homes are open to the public, presenting a lavish show of architectural period styles and personal fancies.

Sugar and slaves enriched Robert Livingston, who owned 160,000 acres in Columbia County. He is more famous, though, for his assistance in the drafting of the Declaration of Independence and as a pioneer of steam navigation. Livingston contracted with inventor Robert Fulton, who built Livingston the 133-foot *Clermont.* The vessel made its maiden voyage in 1807, steaming from New York City to Albany in 28 hours and 45 minutes. A farmer watching the vessel belching smoke from its stack claimed he had "seen the devil going up the river in a sawmill." Livingston's restored mansion, located near Germantown, is now a national historic landmark.

At Staatsburg, Ruth Livingston Mills (a distant relative of Robert Livingston) and her husband, Ogden, hired McKim, Mead & White, the leading architectural firm of the late 19th and early 20th centuries, to design opulent Mills Mansion. The 79-room Beaux Arts showpiece is now open to the public as a state historic site. A tour allows visitors to view the elaborate molded plaster ceilings and marble walls, as well as the home's opulent Louis XIV, XV, and XVI furnishings, including Flemish tapestries in the dining room.

In 1882 Franklin Delano Roosevelt was born in Springwood, a 30-room house south of Hyde Park. Roosevelt's family was long established in the Hudson Valley, owning land in and around Poughkeepsie. FDR's father purchased Springwood in 1867, and the future president and his mother remodeled it in 1915. As president, FDR often spent time at Springwood, using the house as his Election Day headquarters and as a summer White House. The adjacent museum displays many items that trace Roosevelt's political career, including his desk and a specially designed car that permitted the handicapped president to drive guests around his estate. Two miles east of the Roosevelt home stands Val-Kill (Dutch for "valley stream"), a small Dutch-style house used by the family from the 1920's to 1945. After Roosevelt's death in 1945, his wife, Eleanor, made her home here until her death in 1962. Both Roosevelts are buried in the rose garden at Springwood.

as an officer-training school. The academy's illustrious alumni include Ulysses S. Grant, Robert E. Lee, Stonewall Jackson, Philip Sheridan, Douglas MacArthur, and Dwight D. Eisenhower. Visitors can tour the Thayer Museum's fascinating collection of military memorabilia, the restored Fort Putnam, and the Cadet Chapel.

It was during the Revolutionary War that George Washington pronounced West Point "the key to America." Control of the strategic promontory ensured that New England could not be divided from the rest of the colonies. To keep British warships out, Washington commanded his troops to span the river with a 1,500-foot chain made of huge links, each weighing 150 pounds and buoyed on

The Vanderbilt Mansion in Hyde Park is one of the grandest of the Hudson Valley's architectural showplaces. Set on a 200-acre estate once owned by John Jacob Astor, this 54-room Italian Renaissance–style palace was the country retreat of Frederick W. Vanderbilt, son of the legendary New York financier Cornelius Vanderbilt. The house was also built by McKim, Mead & White and completed in 1899. Many of the furnishings and architectural details inside the house were brought over from France, where the Vanderbilt family owned a chateau.

THE KEY TO
AMERICA

At Cold Spring, the Hudson snakes between a promontory and Constitution Island in a sweeping S-curve that takes it past West Point, a great bulge in the river's midsection. Here stands the imposing bulk of the United States Military Academy, founded in 1802

VICTORIAN CHARM
A vestige of bygone days is preserved at one of Cold Spring's lodging houses, below left. Located in the Hudson Highlands, the town boasts a wealth of Victorian architecture.

SLEEPY HOLLOW
The burial ground of Tarrytown's Old Dutch Reformed Church contains the graves of author Washington Irving and philanthropist Andrew Carnegie.

TRACKING THE RIVER
Trains whisk travelers through the Hudson Valley practically at water level. Opposition from canal and steamboat interests delayed railroad construction in the Hudson Valley until the 1840's, when railroad barons began laying track near the waterline, girding both banks of the estuary below Troy.

GILDED AGE
Graceful marble columns frame the spectacular river view from the Vanderbilt Mansion, the 54-room "cottage" built by financier Frederick W. Vanderbilt during the late 1890's.

log rafts. Benedict Arnold, who was commanding the fort, allowed the chain to fall into disrepair as part of his plan to surrender the garrison. Only the timely discovery of his treason saved West Point—and perhaps preserved the young nation's independence. Several links from the original chain can be seen on the grounds of the academy.

TARRY AWHILE Not far from Tarrytown, railroad tycoon Jay Gould made Lyndhurst his summer home from 1880 until his death in 1892. The 30-room, gray stone mansion, capped with spires, battlements, and a tower, is a superb example of the Gothic Revival style. The lavish interior, decorated in silver, brocade, and polished wood, is every bit as impressive as the exterior. Now owned by the National Trust for Historic Preservation, Lyndhurst houses a fine collection of decorative arts from the Victorian period and is surrounded by landscaped grounds.

The bucolic Philipsburg Manor in North Tarrytown is a world away from the opulence of Lyndhurst. Here Frederick Philipse—one of the Hudson's original Dutch patroons—built a mill in about 1680 to grind his tenants' grain and a small house in which to collect their rent. The restored mill, which is still operational, and manor house are the site of demonstrations by guides in period costumes. The manor is also home to a collection of farm animals derived from colonial breeds. These include Gloucester line-back cattle, named for the white line that runs along the animals' spines, and penciled hamburg chickens, which Dutch settlers nicknamed "everyday layers."

Olana, a state historic site south of the Rip Van Winkle Bridge, was once the Moorish castle of artist Frederick E. Church, one of the greatest painters of the Hudson River School. Situated atop a 460-foot hill, Olana was conceived as a living landscape painting, with large windows and doorways to frame sweeping vistas of the river valley. "About an hour this side of Albany is the center of the world," Church wrote. "I own it."

Writer Washington Irving, who peopled the Hudson Valley and the Catskill Mountains with a cast of legendary characters, would probably have understood Church's sentiments. In 1835 Irving purchased Sunnyside, an old Dutch farmstead close to the river. Irving remodeled the house, adding a tower and extra rooms. Today Sunnyside, which contains Irving's extensive library, stands in the shadow of the Tappan Zee Bridge. In *The Legend of Sleepy Hollow*, the author described the view—almost unchanged to this day—that Rip Van Winkle enjoyed before his 20-year nap: "He saw at a distance the lordly Hudson, far, far below him, moving on its silent but majestic course, with the reflection of a purple cloud, or the sail of a lagging bark here and there sleeping on its glassy bosom, and at last losing itself in the blue highlands."

CLERMONT-ON-THE-HUDSON
Seven generations of the Livingston family occupied Clermont, a Georgian mansion built in 1778. Robert Livingston financed inventor Robert Fulton's steamboat, which took its name from the house. Fulton used to dock the vessel at the foot of the property.

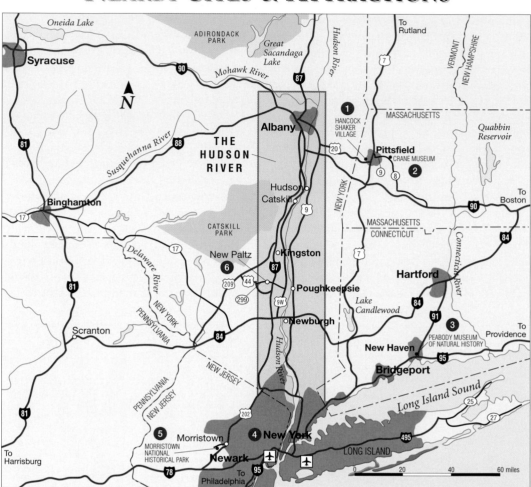

The Round Stone Barn, built in 1826, is a landmark feature of Hancock Shaker Village. The barn's practical design allowed one man to stand in the center of the structure and feed 54 cows at the same time.

1 HANCOCK SHAKER VILLAGE, MASSACHUSETTS

Deep in the scenic Berkshire Hills lies the third of the 18 Shaker communities established in New England, New York, Ohio, and Kentucky between 1776 and 1836. At its peak in the 1830's, Hancock Shaker Village was home to some 300 Shakers. Today the 20 buildings are a museum devoted to the self-sufficient way of life of this fascinating religious sect, whose name derives from the trembling and shaking some members experienced during prayer meetings. Hancock Shaker Village is open daily for self-guided tours from Memorial Day weekend through late October. In April, May, and November, there are guided tours of the main buildings. Located 5 miles west of Pittsfield on Hwy. 20.

2 CRANE MUSEUM, MASSACHUSETTS

Constructed in 1844, this former paper mill is now a museum tracing the history of paper-making in America from the time of the Revolutionary War. Of particular interest are the all-rag papers that Crane and Co. produced for currency, bonds, and stock certificates. The one-story building is located on the banks of the Housatonic River, which supplied the water that washed the rags and drove the machinery of the original mill. The interior of the museum features rough-hewn oak beams, colonial chandeliers, and wide floorboards fastened with wooden dowels. Exhibits include a scale model of the vat process of hand-sheet paper-making. The museum is open Monday to Thursday from June 1 through mid-October. Located in Dalton, 5 miles east of Pittsfield on Hwys. 8 and 9.

3 PEABODY MUSEUM OF NATURAL HISTORY, CONNECTICUT

Yale University's Peabody Museum is one of the oldest university museums of natural history in the United States. The museum's collections were started in 1802 and today contain more than 11 million specimens from the areas of natural history, archeology, and ethnology. The first floor exhibits the museum's huge collection of dinosaur fossils, including the skeleton of a carnivorous dinosaur known as Deinonychus ("terrible claw"), discovered in Montana in 1964. Other displays include 11 wildlife dioramas and artifacts from Meso-America and South America—notably Inca artifacts collected in 1911 from Machu Picchu in Peru by Hiram Bingham. Located at 170 Whitney Ave. in New Haven.

④ NEW YORK CITY

Although the Big Apple boasts a vast range of attractions, the city's fine arts museums rank among the world's most celebrated art collections. On Fifth Avenue's Museum Mile are the Metropolitan Museum of Art, which contains the largest collection of art in the United States; the Guggenheim Museum, where modern European art is housed in an intriguing shell-like building designed by Frank Lloyd Wright; and the Frick Collection, made up almost entirely of European works from the 16th to the 19th centuries. The Museum of Modern Art, affectionately known as MOMA, contains a magnificent collection that includes works by Picasso, Matisse, van Gogh, Monet, and Pollock, as well as a world-famous design collection. The Whitney Museum of American Art is a work of art in itself: its cantilevered structure is one of the city's boldest architectural designs. The Whitney's collection represents the full range of 20th-century American art.

⑤ MORRISTOWN NATIONAL HISTORICAL PARK, NEW JERSEY

During the Revolutionary War, George Washington and his troops spent the bitter winter of 1779-80 in Morristown. General Washington and his aides-de-camp were billeted in the home of Mrs. Jacob Ford, Jr., while his troops camped in nearby Jockey Hollow. Morristown National Historical Park preserves the Georgian-style Ford mansion, as well as the site of the Jockey Hollow encampment. The Ford House has been restored and visitors can view the rooms Washington used to conduct military business; a film portrays the life led by the 10,000 soldiers of the Continental Army, who spent the winter—one of the century's worst—huddled in log huts. Some of these huts have been reconstructed at the Jockey Hollow site, now a tranquil 1,319-acre park. Located 6 miles outside Morristown.

⑥ NEW PALTZ, NEW YORK

When a group of Huguenot families arrived in the Hudson Valley in 1677, they named their settlement New Paltz, after the town on the Rhine River where other French Protestants had found refuge from persecution. Many of the steep-roofed, one-room stone houses built by the new arrivals after 1692 still line New Paltz's Huguenot Street, which is said to be the oldest street in America that still contains its original houses. Visitors can tour these houses, which are maintained by the Huguenot Historical Society. The house of Jean Housbrouck, which displays family furniture, china, clothing, toys, and portraits, is considered to be the most outstanding example of medieval Flemish stone architecture in America. Located west of Hwy. 87 on Hwy. 299.

Pittsburgh businessman Henry Clay Frick built this mansion on New York's Fifth Avenue to house his celebrated collection of painting, sculpture, furniture, and decorative arts. Today the Frick Collection is one of the highlights of Manhattan's Museum Mile.

THE BLUE RIDGE PARKWAY

*America's oldest rural parkway skirts
along the untamed peaks of the
Appalachian Mountains.*

In the dark days of the Great Depression, the idea of building a scenic highway that would skim the southern Appalachian mountain peaks for almost 500 uninterrupted miles seemed about as realistic as the Hollywood musicals of the day. Such a fantasy was fun to think about and could, like the movies, take people's minds off the hard times around them. But nobody could ever truly build such a road. Or could they?

Franklin D. Roosevelt must have thought otherwise. In 1933 the president visited a construction site in the new Shenandoah National Park, authorized in the flush times of 1926. The now-legendary Civilian Conservation Corps (CCC) was carving out a section of road along the crest of the Blue Ridge Mountains. That pioneering roadway, the Skyline Drive, eventually would traverse the new park for 105

miles. But in 1933 most of it was incomplete; in fact, the entire mountain region thereabouts was a mess. Years of reckless logging, mining, and subsistence farming had produced an eroded, used-up wasteland. Shenandoah National Park was more about reclamation than preservation.

According to National Park Service lore, a member of the president's party that day suggested to FDR that the road ought to continue southwest beyond the borders of Shenandoah National Park all the way to the Great Smoky Mountains National Park—a breathtaking ramble of 469 additional miles. The idea appealed to the ever-positive FDR and, later in the year, $16 million was budgeted for a new highway that would run through the states of Virginia and North Carolina and be called the Blue Ridge Parkway.

The eager states donated the right-of-way to the National Park Service, and the wretched economic times were, perversely, an asset: men were desperate for work and contractors were starved for new projects. An alphabet soup of federal and state government agencies smoothed the way in a Depression-born spirit of cooperation. Construction began in September 1935 along a 12-mile stretch near the Virginia–North Carolina border. Even the outbreak of World War II did not

shut the work down entirely. Work camps of conscientious objectors kept the project going. It was not until 1987, however, that the dramatic Linn Cove Viaduct was completed along the rocky flanks of Grandfather Mountain in North Carolina, connecting the great road at last.

DESIGNED FOR MOTORISTS

Nowadays more than 27,000 visitors enjoy some portion of the parkway daily, a small percentage of whom may cover the entire distance in a single spurt. At a maximum 45 miles an hour, the trip takes at least 11 or 12 hours if the road is uncluttered by man, beast, winter storm, or sudden impenetrable fog (a year-round possibility), but the effort seems rather senseless. The point of a drive on the Blue Ridge Parkway is not to get anywhere, but to enjoy the natural beauty, local color, and regional history encountered along the way. It's a shame—as well as risky—to rush a trip on the parkway. The gently banked, curvy, two-lane road just isn't built for speed.

From the zero milepost, just above Waynesboro, Virginia, at the intersection of Interstate 64, the road follows the crest of the Blue Ridge Mountains for 340 miles, sometimes tracing a straight line,

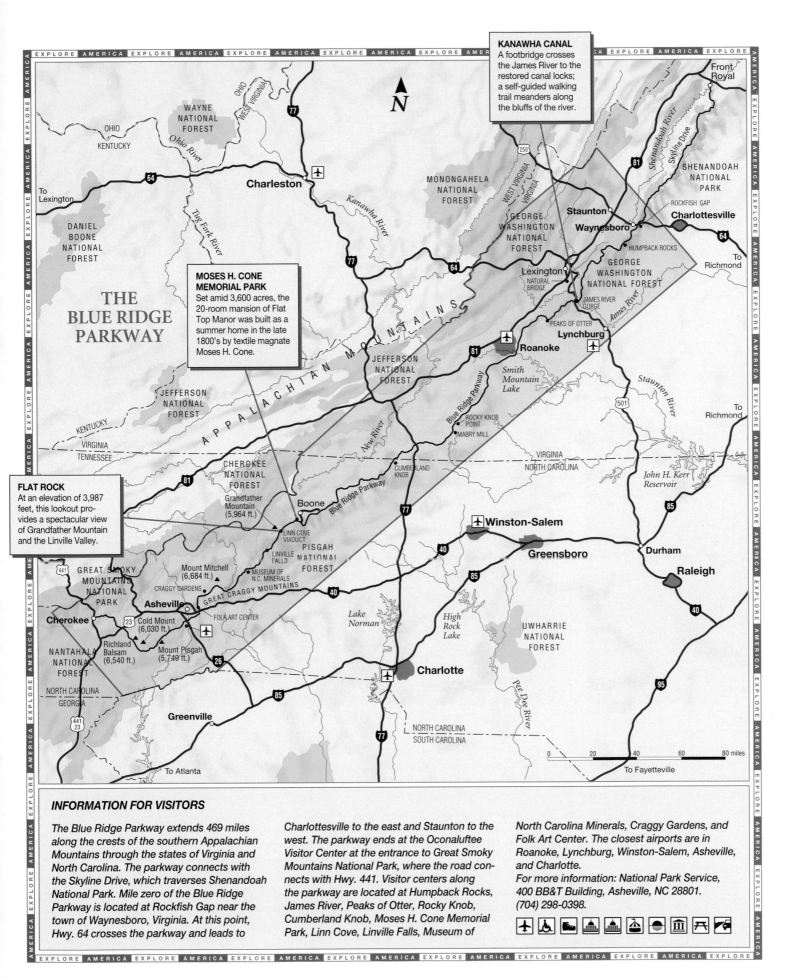

KANAWHA CANAL
A footbridge crosses the James River to the restored canal locks; a self-guided walking trail meanders along the bluffs of the river.

MOSES H. CONE MEMORIAL PARK
Set amid 3,600 acres, the 20-room mansion of Flat Top Manor was built as a summer home in the late 1800's by textile magnate Moses H. Cone.

FLAT ROCK
At an elevation of 3,987 feet, this lookout provides a spectacular view of Grandfather Mountain and the Linville Valley.

THE BLUE RIDGE PARKWAY

Front Royal

Charleston

WAYNE NATIONAL FOREST

OHIO
KENTUCKY

Ohio River

To Lexington

DANIEL BOONE NATIONAL FOREST

Tug Fork River

Kanawha River

MONONGAHELA NATIONAL FOREST

WEST VIRGINIA
VIRGINIA

GEORGE WASHINGTON NATIONAL FOREST

Shenandoah River

Skyline Drive

SHENANDOAH NATIONAL PARK

ROCKFISH GAP

Staunton
Waynesboro
Charlottesville

HUMPBACK ROCKS

To Richmond

Lexington
NATURAL BRIDGE

GEORGE WASHINGTON NATIONAL FOREST

JAMES RIVER GORGE

PEAKS OF OTTER

Lynchburg

James River

APPALACHIAN MOUNTAINS

JEFFERSON NATIONAL FOREST

Smith Mountain Lake

Roanoke

Blue Ridge Parkway

ROCKY KNOB POINT
MABRY MILL

Staunton River

To Richmond

JEFFERSON NATIONAL FOREST

KENTUCKY
VIRGINIA
TENNESSEE

New River

Boone

CUMBERLAND KNOB

VIRGINIA
NORTH CAROLINA

John H. Kerr Reservoir

CHEROKEE NATIONAL FOREST

Grandfather Mountain (5,964 ft.)

LINN COVE VIADUCT

LINVILLE FALLS

Blue Ridge Parkway

PISGAH NATIONAL FOREST

Winston-Salem

Greensboro

Durham

Raleigh

GREAT SMOKY MOUNTAINS NATIONAL PARK

Mount Mitchell (6,684 ft.)
CRAGGY GARDENS
MUSEUM OF N.C. MINERALS

GREAT CRAGGY MOUNTAINS

Asheville
FOLK ART CENTER

Lake Norman

High Rock Lake

UWHARRIE NATIONAL FOREST

Cherokee
Cold Mount (6,030 ft.)

NANTAHALA NATIONAL FOREST

Richland Balsam (6,540 ft.)
Mount Pisgah (5,749 ft.)

Charlotte

NORTH CAROLINA
GEORGIA

Greenville

Pee Dee River

NORTH CAROLINA
SOUTH CAROLINA

To Atlanta

0   20   40   60   80 miles

To Fayetteville

INFORMATION FOR VISITORS

The Blue Ridge Parkway extends 469 miles along the crests of the southern Appalachian Mountains through the states of Virginia and North Carolina. The parkway connects with the Skyline Drive, which traverses Shenandoah National Park. Mile zero of the Blue Ridge Parkway is located at Rockfish Gap near the town of Waynesboro, Virginia. At this point, Hwy. 64 crosses the parkway and leads to

Charlottesville to the east and Staunton to the west. The parkway ends at the Oconaluftee Visitor Center at the entrance to Great Smoky Mountains National Park, where the road connects with Hwy. 441. Visitor centers along the parkway are located at Humpback Rocks, James River, Peaks of Otter, Rocky Knob, Cumberland Knob, Moses H. Cone Memorial Park, Linn Cove, Linville Falls, Museum of

North Carolina Minerals, Craggy Gardens, and Folk Art Center. The closest airports are in Roanoke, Lynchburg, Winston-Salem, Asheville, and Charlotte.
For more information: National Park Service, 400 BB&T Building, Asheville, NC 28801. (704) 298-0398.

Pink azalea shrubs cling to moss-coated boulders near Linville Falls, seen in the background at right. The Linville River snakes through a forest of hemlock and towering white pine trees before cascading to the bottom of Linville Gorge.

LOCAL RESIDENT
The eastern chipmunk, below, is a denizen of the forests cloaking the Appalachian Mountains, which were once the habitat of wolves, elk, buffalo, and mountain lions. Black bears still can be sighted here.

sometimes tweaking a driver's sense of direction in a confusing, disorganized tumble of mountains. At points in southern Virginia, the craggy wilderness seems to suddenly recede, replaced by a gently rolling rural landscape of cornfields and pastures. But soon the mountains resume in earnest, building up to Mount Mitchell, the highest peak in eastern North America. By now the parkway has left the Blue Ridge (which has wandered off to the south) and, with another 114 miles to go, has entered the Black Mountains. These soon give way to the Great Craggy Mountains, which in turn give way to the Balsams, before the Great Smokies loom ahead at the end of the road. The drive's average elevation is between 3,000 and 4,000 feet—high enough to be

cool when it's sweltering down below. The lowest point is the James River Gorge, where the river makes its age-old turn from the mountainous west into the open Piedmont at a mere 650-foot elevation. The road's highest point is at 6,047 feet, on the flanks of a mountain called Richland Balsam, located west of Asheville, North Carolina.

With more than 250 overlooks along the parkway, if motorists miss one view, there's sure to be another just down the road. These often seem to hang in space, and indeed two of these—Raven's Roost and Roanoke Mountain—are used as launching pads by hang-gliding enthusiasts, who take their cue from the hawks and ravens that soar in the thermals that waft upward at certain spots.

Other stopping points access easy hiking trails to natural wonders, such as dramatic Linville Falls, which John D. Rockefeller bought and donated to the parkway.

Wilderness it is, but a convenient wilderness. Scattered along the route, six National Park Service visitor centers dispense information on the parkway, and each one concentrates on some aspect of the region's natural and human history.

Winter drives on the parkway can be magnificent. Distances often seem magnified in the absence of leaf cover, and the mountains take on a majestic stillness, like waves of a frozen ocean. But keep in mind that sudden snows, freezes, and fogbanks may be real perils, and entire sections of the road are often closed. Most visitors come from the beginning of May through October when all facilities are open and there is an endless, rotating panoply of colorful trees, shrubs, blossoms, and wildflowers. The white lace of dogwood makes its shy appearance late in April, frosting the otherwise bare forest, a signal for greening to begin. Then come the blossoms of white Fraser magnolia, flame azalea, and the pale pink of mountain laurel. To many observers, the chief blooming glory of the region is the rhododendron, whose dense, dark-green masses explode in early June with purple and red blossoms. Naturally the schedule runs behind concentrations of rhododendron at higher elevations such as spectacular Craggy Gardens in the lofty Balsams of North Carolina. Soon it will be early October, when the spectacle of fall foliage begins. This is the time when the forests take center stage with their brilliant displays of red, yellow, and orange.

Traces of the original settlers in these southern Appalachians are here for those who seek them, interpreted by the National Park Service. At the parkway's northern end, the Humpback Rocks Visitor Center features a mountain farm museum, complete with log house and outbuildings. The reconstruction demonstrates that despite a sublime setting, subsistence life in these mountains was no easy matter. About 170 miles farther south, in southern Virginia, stands one of the parkway's most popular sights—an authentic mountain gristmill known as Mabry Mill. Demonstrations of flour grinding and blacksmithing occur here in season.

WATER POWER
Mabry Mill was built by and run by Ed Mabry from 1910 to 1935. The mill complex included a blacksmith shop, gristmill, sawmill, and a woodworking shop.

institution can be first-class fun. Scattered across rolling grounds of nearly 200 acres is a collection of centuries-old cottages and farm buildings from England, Ireland, Germany, and the Appalachian frontier itself. The idea is to tell the story—through authentic structures and costumed interpreters—of the 18th-century Europeans who were the primary settlers of the Appalachian frontier. The visitor comes away with a better understanding of the complexity and mobility of immigrant society, especially that formidable group known as the Scotch-Irish, who settled Augusta and Rockbridge counties. Among their descendants who went on to glory were Sam Houston and Woodrow Wilson.

Lexington, Virginia—sometimes called the Valhalla of the Confederacy—rivals Staunton as a cultural center and picturesque town. Two of America's most beautiful and historic colleges have

adjoining campuses here. At Washington and Lee University, founded in 1749, the presence of Robert E. Lee still seems to walk beside the white columns of W&L's colonnaded architecture. At Virginia Military Institute, Stonewall Jackson was teaching on campus when the Civil War began. Among its distinguished alumni is George C. Marshall, chief of staff of the army during World War II and author of the postwar Marshall Plan. The VMI Museum, Lee Chapel, and the Marshall Library and Research Center are important stops for anyone with an interest in modern American history.

| ROANOKE AND BEYOND | The parkway brushes the edge of the western Virginia city of Roanoke. In the downtown area of this lively city is Center in the Square, a cultural complex that includes museums of fine art, history, and science, as well as the performing arts. The Virginia Transportation Museum is the final resting place of a group of |

DOWN IN THE VALLEY
An overlook, above, provides a spectacular view of the forested Shenandoah Valley.

BERRY SEASON
The bright red berries, right, of the elderberry shrub, which ripen at the beginning of September, are used to make wine and jellies.

A more sophisticated demonstration of mountain culture takes place beside the parkway above Asheville, where the Folk Art Center features choice mountain crafts from nine Appalachian states. Artisans produce traditional wares such as brooms, dulcimers, and quilts on the premises; contemporary crafts on sale in the center's galleries include ceramics, wood carvings, furniture, fabrics, and stained glass.

Beyond such roadside attractions lie some of the southern Appalachians' most intriguing institutions. Consider Staunton, Virginia, whose winking lights brighten the evening landscape down in the Shenandoah Valley. Here the Museum of American Frontier Culture shows that a serious

behemoths of the age of steam, a time when Roanoke was an important railway center. The reopening in 1995 of the lavishly restored Hotel Roanoke, a world-famous institution since the 1880's, was an auspicious event. A local landmark, the Tudor-style hotel occupies its own hill in the center of town.

The towns of western North Carolina that fall within the orbit of the Blue Ridge Parkway are linked by one predominant feature: a generations-long association with vacationers. The region's extreme elevations and tumbled, steep-flanked mountains make it ideal ski country. The town of Boone, with its 3,333-foot elevation, is the hub of many of North Carolina's ski areas, as well as resorts for all seasons.

One of the most beautifully situated cities in the world, Asheville, North Carolina, rests lightly between the Blue Ridge and the Great Smokies, surrounded by misty ranges whose tint runs to blues and purples. Native son and novelist Thomas Wolfe described himself as one "hill-bound, sky-girt, of whom the mountains were his masters." Even though the town has changed since Wolfe's early 20th-century boyhood, the most important structure in his greatest works remains just as it was in the years before World War I: his mother's rambling, gabled boarding house, eerily untouched by time, is now the Thomas Wolfe Memorial State Historic Site. For anyone who has read *Look Homeward, Angel*, it's a spine-tingling experience to wander through the battered interior and conjure up scenes from the novel that burst into the mind with three-dimensional clarity.

"Great things are done when men and mountains meet," wrote the 19th-century poet William Blake. He might have been speaking of the Blue Ridge Parkway itself.

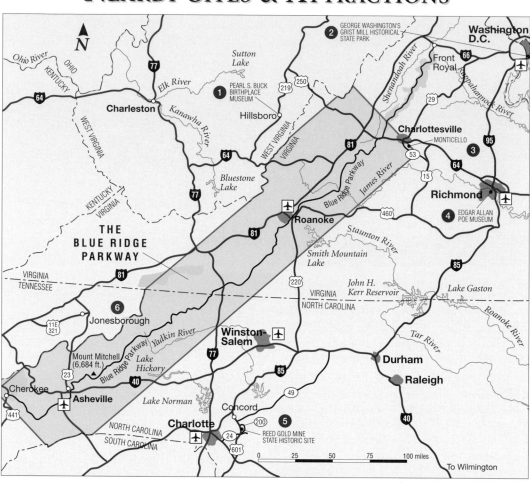

The gristmill rebuilt by George Washington harnessed the waters of Dogue Run and was used to grind grain into flour. The mill was reconstructed in the 1930's.

① PEARL S. BUCK BIRTHPLACE MUSEUM, WEST VIRGINIA

The birthplace of Pearl S. Buck—the first American woman writer to win both the Pulitzer and Nobel prizes—is a fitting memorial to an author whose novels, such as *The Good Earth*, helped to foster understanding between China and the West. The house was built by Buck's grandfather during the 1840's, and she was born here in 1892 while her parents were on leave from missionary work in China. With its balconied portico, the gracious house has been meticulously restored and contains furnishings that the author knew as a child. These include an 1857 organ and her grandfather's bed, made from cherrywood fenceposts. Displays include photographs of the author during her childhood years. Located in Hillsboro on Route 219.

② GEORGE WASHINGTON'S GRIST MILL HISTORICAL STATE PARK, VIRGINIA

In 1761 Washington inherited the Mount Vernon estate from his half-brother, which included a decrepit gristmill. Washington built a new mill and oversaw its operation for the rest of his life. After his death, the mill eventually fell into disrepair. Visitors can tour the reconstruction, which is a faithful replica of the mill that Washington built, and learn how an

18th-century gristmill ground wheat into flour. The breast-shot waterwheel, which was powered by water flowing from a mill pond, is located on the ground floor along with two sets of millstones. Also on view are the conveyors that took the flour to sifting and storage areas on the upper two stories. Located 3 miles west of the Mount Vernon Estate on Mount Vernon Memorial Hwy.

③ MONTICELLO, VIRGINIA

Thomas Jefferson built a house atop a mountain that was part of his inheritance, and named it Monticello, which means "little mountain" in Italian. Work on the original house began in 1769, but Jefferson was never entirely satisfied with the results. After a five-year sojourn in France, he decided to redesign Monticello along the neoclassical lines that were then popular in Europe. Jefferson tore down sections of the house and rebuilt them, adding a single classical portico and a dome—the first ever built in Virginia. Today the house stands as a testament to Jefferson's ingenuity and architectural vision. The first-floor entrance hall contains a collection of paintings and fossils, as well as objects collected by the Lewis and Clark expedition. A seven-day calendar clock over the main door was designed by Jefferson himself. The dining room features a dumbwaiter that delivered wine from the cellar and a revolving door with shelves that facilitated the serving of meals. Located 3 miles southeast of Charlottesville on Hwy. 53.

4 EDGAR ALLAN POE MUSEUM, VIRGINIA

Devoted to the life and career of writer Edgar Allan Poe—author of *The Fall of the House of Usher*—the museum occupies five buildings in Richmond, the city in which Poe spent most of his life. One of these buildings, the 1737 Old Stone House, is the oldest structure in Richmond. The museum features the largest collection of Poe memorabilia in the world, including original letters and manuscripts, first editions, and photographs and paintings of Poe's family and friends. The Raven Room displays illustrations of Poe's poem *The Raven*. The Enchanted Garden, behind the Old Stone House, exhibits Poe's favorite flowers and plants. Located at 1914-16 East Main Street in Richmond.

5 REED GOLD MINE STATE HISTORIC SITE, NORTH CAROLINA

Until the 1840's, North Carolina was the nation's leading gold producer. This state historic site marks the spot of the first authenticated gold find and the first gold mine in the United States. Visitors may explore mine tunnels running 50 feet underground, pan for gold, and meander along walking trails to view the old mine shafts. A visitor center houses gold artifacts and mining equipment from the Reed mine, where 12-year-old Conrad Reed found a 17-pound gold nugget on his father's farm in 1799. The family unwittingly used the massive nugget as a doorstop until they sold it to a local jeweler for

$3.50. In 1803 the Reeds began mining in earnest and, in the process, extracted the largest nugget ever found on the East Coast: it weighed 28 pounds. Located 7 miles south of Concord on Hwy. 200.

6 JONESBOROUGH, TENNESSEE

With the coming of the railroad, this town—the oldest in Tennessee—became a prosperous transportation center. Today Jonesborough's historic district boasts a fine collection of architectural treasures from this era. Among them are the town's oldest building—the 1797 Chester Inn—and the stately courthouse, built on the site of Jonesborough's original log cabin courthouse. Tours of the historic district begin at the History Museum, where displays featuring pioneer tools, building techniques, early trades, and transportation help to trace the community's development. Located on Hwys. 11E and 321.

A lifelike rendering of the face of Edgar Allan Poe at Richmond's Poe Museum commemorates this master of the macabre. Poe lived in Richmond for most of his life.

On his estate at Monticello, Thomas Jefferson was able to indulge his passion for gardening. The result is a delightful collection of formal and vegetable gardens.

THE OVERSEAS HIGHWAY

*Thirty-six islands of the Florida Keys,
linked by 43 bridges, make up
this highway to the sea.*

In the early hours of dawn, the waters encompassing the Florida Keys are slightly opaque, as if blanketed by a thin cloak of fog. Approaching mid-morning the intensity of the sun draws the drab pigments into astoundingly rich hues: a dark velvet blue in the offshore Gulf Stream, a lime-turquoise in the shallows, and a rippling reflection of blinding white at the shoreline. The pace of life in the Keys tends to mirror this daily pattern of gradual, soothing unfoldment.

This chain of islands curves out into the Gulf of Mexico like carefully placed stepping stones, extending 126 miles from the Florida mainland and ending just short of Cuba. Although their beauty is acknowledged the world over, the first European explorers viewed them differently. In 1513 Ponce de Leon's expedition labeled them Los Martires ("the martyrs") because from a distance the low-lying, rocky islands "appeared like men who were suffering." Later, less gloomy Spanish explorers called

BEACH BREAK
A stretch of sandy beach dotted with tropical palm trees beckons visitors to relax and take advantage of the slower pace of island life. Bahia Honda has one of the finest beaches in the Keys.

AN ISLAND CHAIN
Overleaf: This string of tiny islands, some of which are linked together by the Overseas Highway, arc out from the Florida mainland into the Gulf of Mexico. Their unique location provides the Keys with a temperate climate year-round.

them cayos huesos ("bone keys") from which the city of Key West is derived. Originally a haven for pirates, the Keys became the wrecking ground for Spanish treasure ships, then home to British Loyalists who fled the American Revolution. The man who helped turn them into one of the world's premier water parks was the same single-minded railroad tycoon who opened up the rest of South Florida, Henry M. Flagler.

FROM RAIL TO ROAD

In 1905 Flagler decided to extend his rail line from Homestead, Florida, to the deep-water port of Key West. The port of Miami had only a 12-foot clearance in Biscayne Bay, which was too shallow for big ships. At the age of 75, Flagler undertook the seven-year task of building what some detractors called "the railroad that went to the sea." Despite the deaths of hundreds of workers and tremendous destruction caused by hurricanes, Flagler's crews constructed the 43 bridges needed to reach Key West, including the "Big One"—seven miles long—over open water. Justifiably proud, Flagler rolled into Key West on January 22, 1912, in a grand railway coach.

Before bridges connected the islands, traveling in the Keys had been limited to sailing, rowing, or poling. The arrival of the railroad altered life in the Keys forever, as did its dramatic disappearance. Many predicted that a storm would one day kill Flagler's railroad, and they were right. On Labor Day, 1935, an unnamed hurricane with winds in excess of 200 miles an hour drove a 17-foot-high wall of water across the low-lying Keys, causing 700 deaths and knocking the train off the tracks.

Although the train and the railroad were destroyed, every one of Flagler's bridges withstood the storm. His construction engineers had created remarkable, enduring monuments. And those brave enough to remain in the Keys knew exactly how to take advantage of the structures. In 1938

INFORMATION FOR VISITORS

The Overseas Highway, Hwy. 1, connects with Hwy. 95 at Miami; in Homestead, Hwy. 1 connects with the Florida's Turnpike extension. After crossing Barnes Sound, the highway leads onto Key Largo, the first island in the Keys, which is located 42 miles southwest of Miami. Mile markers, often referred to as mile posts, line the right shoulder of the highway. These small green signs with prominent white numbers begin with number 126, south of Florida City. The zero mile marker is located at the corner of Fleming and Whitehead streets in downtown Key West. The closest scheduled commercial air service is into Miami, Marathon, and Key West.

For more information: Florida Keys & Key West Visitors Bureau, P.O. Box 1147, Key West, FL 33041. (305) 296-1552 or (800)-FLA-KEYS.

STANDING SENTINEL
Fishing for dinner in the Keys is easy for anglers and seabirds alike. The abundance of fish attracts white herons, roseate spoonbills, pelicans, seagulls, ospreys, and snowy egrets, like the one shown above.

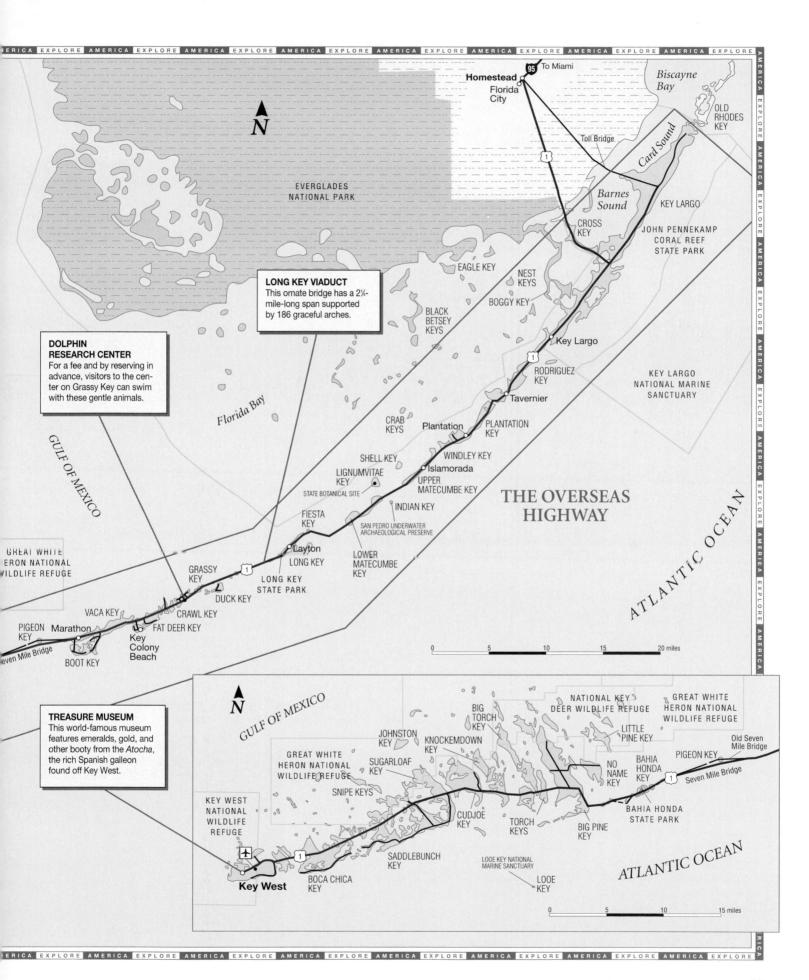

LONG KEY VIADUCT
This ornate bridge has a 2¼-mile-long span supported by 186 graceful arches.

DOLPHIN RESEARCH CENTER
For a fee and by reserving in advance, visitors to the center on Grassy Key can swim with these gentle animals.

TREASURE MUSEUM
This world-famous museum features emeralds, gold, and other booty from the *Atocha*, the rich Spanish galleon found off Key West.

THE OVERSEAS HIGHWAY

REEF PATROL

A school of blue-striped grunts enjoys the clear waters of John Pennekamp Coral Reef State Park and the Key Largo National Marine Sanctuary. The preserves are home to more than 500 species of tropical fish and 55 types of Atlantic coral. To get a glimpse of life beneath the surface, underwater enthusiasts can scuba dive, snorkel, or take a ride in a glass-bottom boat.

ANGLERS' DELIGHT

In 1982, 37 of the 43 bridges that link the Keys were replaced with sturdier spans. Off-limits to motorists, many of the old bridges jut into the sea and make ideal perches for anglers. The old Seven Mile Bridge at Marathon, right, is the world's longest fishing pier.

just three years after the devastating no-name hurricane, the railway route was reopened. The rails were still there—they now function as guard rails—but the bed was paved over for automobiles. The former Overseas Railroad had been resourcefully converted into the Overseas Highway, an extension of the nation's main East Coast road, U.S. 1.

The old railroad bed continued to serve as the foundation of U.S. 1 until 1982, when many of the narrow, deteriorating sections were repaired or replaced altogether with wider, more modern bridges. The practice of gauging distance by mile markers—a system first introduced by Flagler's railroad—is still in use today. Mile marker 0 stands prominently in Key West.

TRAVELING BY MILE MARKER

Locals divide the Keys into three geographic regions: the Upper, Middle, and Lower Keys. More than distance separates the regions, as visitors who drive the full length of Highway 1 discover. The mindset of Key Largo is entirely different from that of Key West.

Mile marker 109 in Key Largo is the spot where U.S. 1 officially joins the Florida Keys. Key Largo is

essentially composed of hard coral rock bordered in many places by thick ribbons of mangrove trees. Because of these characteristics, Key Largo was originally called Rock Harbor, a tiny settlement with a post office on the outskirts of present-day Key Largo.

If the town of Key Largo initially disappoints because it looks like "Anywhere U.S.A.," it helps to remember that land-based activities are not what draw people here from all over the world. Water is the lure: Key Largo is headquarters of the John Pennekamp Coral Reef State Park, an underwater wonderland with 500 different species of fish, including neon-colored queen angels, red snapper, and spotted grouper, and more than 55 types of Atlantic coral. Florida has the only true coral reef system in all of North America. Functioning as an important nursery for many species of game fish as well as the chief residence of bottom dwellers, this living barrier reef system is arguably the state's greatest natural treasure. The park also features a 4,000-pound bronze statue called "Christ of the Deep." The shrine, located 25 feet under water, sits on a 20-ton concrete base.

If Key Largo's marine sanctuary is a magnet for underwater enthusiasts, then Islamorada ("purple isle") is a mecca for serious anglers. Islamorada (pronounced *eye-lah-more-AH-da*) includes Plantation, Windley, and Matecumbe keys, extending roughly from mile marker 90 to mile marker 63. Because it has always harbored the largest number

of charter boats anywhere in the Keys, Islamorada has rightfully billed itself for decades as the "Sportfishing Capital of the World." One of the most sought-after game fish here is the bonefish, which tends to be a resident of the Gulf side, referred to as Florida Bay or the "back country." On the Atlantic side, large sportfishing boats 30 feet and longer employ flying bridges and downriggers to search the nearby Gulf Stream for the big game that feed here: sailfish, possibly even a marlin or swordfish.

The Keys are often referred to as America's version of the Caribbean, and this is not an undue description. Many plants that grow in the Keys today originate from seeds carried to these islands from the Caribbean by wind and waves. Perhaps the best place to witness the Keys of a hundred years ago is at the Lignumvitae Key State Botanical Site, near mile marker 79, between Upper and Lower

VERDANT VEGETATION
Sunlight filters through the swaying branches of a gumbo-limbo tree adorned with blooming cacti. Known to locals as the "tourist tree," because its red bark resembles the skin of sunburned visitors, the tree is just one of many different species of tropical vegetation that thrive on Lignumvitae Key.

The National Key Deer Refuge on Big Pine Key provides a safe haven for Key deer, right, which grow to be no larger than a medium-size dog and weigh between 45 and 75 pounds. A newborn fawn weighs two to four pounds, and its hoof is the size of a human thumbnail. The deer are most easily seen at sunrise and sunset.

Ernest Hemingway's house and gardens, located at the corner of Whitehead and Olivia streets, are one of Key West's most popular attractions. Hemingway lived in the house for about 10 years before he moved to Cuba. Local legend has it that the six-toed cats that roam the gardens are direct descendants of Hemingway's pets.

Matecumbe Keys. Lignumvitae Key, a mile offshore, can be reached only by boat. This 280-acre island not only enjoys one of the highest elevations in the Keys, but also contains Florida's last virgin stands of tropical hammocks of typical West Indian trees, including the endangered lignumvitae tree (Latin for "wood of life"). This incredibly durable hardwood deserves its name: the tree supposedly can live a thousand years. Overall, an estimated 133 different kinds of trees, including banyan, gumbo-limbo, mastic, strangler fig, sapodilla, and poisonwood (which closely resembles lignumvitae), flourish on Lignumvitae Key.

Located just a mile south of Indian Key is the San Pedro Underwater Archaeological Preserve, where the remains of a wrecked Spanish galleon lie in only 18 feet of water. The 287-foot *San Pedro* sank in a 1733 hurricane. Original ballast stones, anchors, and seven concrete cannon replicas are on exhibit.

The Long Key State Recreation Area, a narrow ribbon of beach fronting the Atlantic, is one of the finest camping areas in the Keys. The campsites are shaded by tall Australian pines, whose rustling in the frequent breeze is guaranteed to lull any camper to sleep. Day visitors have the option of picnicking overlooking the water or hiking on two excellent nature trails.

Every activity for which the Florida Keys are famed is readily available in the Upper Keys, so the majority of visitors never travel as far as the Middle or Lower Keys. Those who decide to go the extra distance generally find less crowded conditions.

Marathon—the self-described "Heart of the Keys"—is another booming fishing and diving center. At mile marker 50, right in the middle of Marathon, is one of the Keys' most environmentally sensitive and important archeological sites: the 63.5-acre Crane Point Hammock. Here is found North America's sole

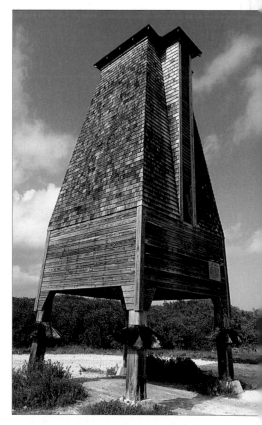

remaining virgin palm hammock, as well as evidence of at least 5,000 years of habitation, including pre-Columbian and prehistoric Bahamian artifacts. The Museum of Natural History of the Florida Keys and a separate children's museum offer both permanent and temporary exhibits on the region's geography, botany, and zoology.

There are two Seven Mile bridges jutting from Marathon today. Flagler's original, built of concrete imported from Germany, is predominantly a fishing pier, although anglers share it with joggers, campers, in-line skaters, and anyone else who can think of a good excuse for being on a bridge that no longer goes anywhere.

The newer Seven Mile Bridge runs from mile marker 47 to mile marker 40—an honest and true seven miles—to enter the Lower Keys. Just after mile marker 37, Bahia Honda State Park is part of

the geological transition zone where a limestone substance called oolite now layers the hard coral base. (Oolite, which resembles tiny fish eggs, is also the main base underlying the mainland Everglades.) Visitors may not be aware of any geological changes, but they can easily detect that the Lower Keys are different in several significant ways. Bahia Honda State Park, for instance, offers what many visitors would by now never expect to see: a large, wonderful sand beach accompanied by something even more remarkable—sand dunes. Big Pine Key is notable for its small population of the tiny Key deer, which are making their final stand in Big Pine's National Key Deer Refuge. These miniature creatures, once common on many of the Keys, today number only between 250 and 300. Before leaving Big Pine Key, visitors should consider taking a boat ride to Looe Key National Marine

VINTAGE CHARM

Southernmost House is a fine example of the "Conch" style of architecture unique to the Keys. This two-and-a-half-story wooden structure was erected during Key West's golden age in the 19th century. Its exterior embellishments include gingerbread trim, verandas, and turrets—all decked out in pastel colors.

Sanctuary. These offshore shallow reefs rival many of Pennekamp's more popular sites.

The largest city of the island chain is Key West. A colorful combination of Southern, Bahamian, Cuban, and Yankee influences is visible in the architecture, savored in the local cuisine, and felt in the relaxed atmosphere.

Long-time Key Westers call themselves "Conchs" (pronounced *konks*), the nickname given Loyalists who fled to the Bahamas during the American Revolution. Many moved to Key West, where they were employed as wreckers, who salvaged the numerous ships that piled up on the reefs.

WRITERS AND SUN WORSHIPERS

Once primarily a day trip for those staying in the Upper and Middle Keys, the city of Key West is now an important tourist destination, receiving about 1 million visitors a year. Regrettably, those who come to experience the free-wheeling Key West lifestyle, epitomized by the novelist Ernest Hemingway, are a few decades too late. Although the hard-drinking, hard-fishing writer is closely identified with Key West, other important people are immortalized here as well. Famed naturalist John James Audubon painted local birds in Key West in 1831 and 1832, staying in Audubon House on Washington Street, which was the property of Capt. John Geiger at the time. Pres. Harry Truman established his own Little White House in Key West during his term in office.

Lacking, for the most part, the name of any famous resident are the many 19th-century homes in Old Town, which bear 60 different gingerbread designs in elaborately turned railings and eaves. Some of the most popular shapes are Grecian urns, wine bottles, hearts, and ships' wheels.

A day in Key West may be spent diving, fishing, or just lolling on the beach, but the early evening belongs to Mallory Square pier. That's where locals and visitors alike gather for Key West's greatest spectacle: the celebration of the setting sun. Sunset is an elaborate daily ritual that begins with jugglers, magicians, and local politicians, who all turn out to entertain the crowd at daylight's final hours. Although the street theater doesn't cost a cent, many performers do solicit donations—some more insistently than others.

Still, it's the sunset everyone comes to behold, and no one leaves disappointed. Sighs of appreciation are to be expected, but there are few places in the world where the setting sun routinely draws a standing ovation from the crowd.

HEMINGWAY'S HANGOUT
Key West's most famous resident liked to hang out in Captain Tony's Saloon, originally called Sloppy Joe's. A great place to soak up the local atmosphere, the interior of the bar is wallpapered in business cards and newspaper clippings.

SOUTHERNMOST SUNSETS
The sun sinks slowly into the turquoise waters of the Gulf of Mexico, bathing the sky with fiery red and luminous golden swathes of color.

39

A strangler fig insidiously wraps its branches around the trunk of a host tree in Florida's Corkscrew Swamp Sanctuary. A fully grown strangler fig may eventually overwhelm its host.

NEARBY SITES & ATTRACTIONS

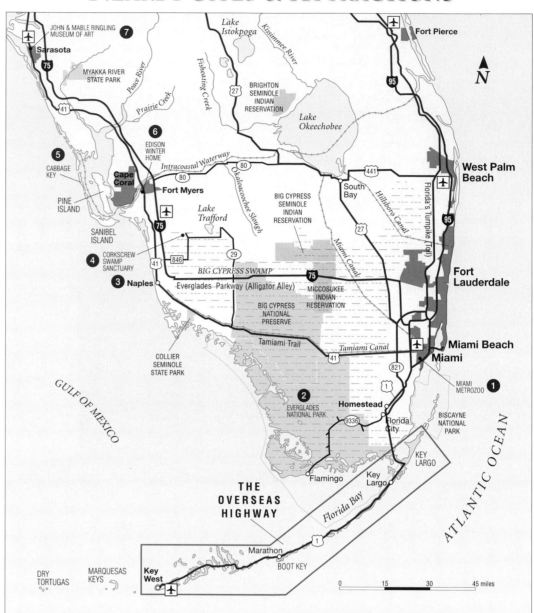

① MIAMI METROZOO

Spread over 290 acres, Miami's sprawling MetroZoo has one of the world's largest collections of animals in captivity, featuring some 1,000 animals from every continent. The zoo is dedicated to the conservation and preservation of endangered species, including the rare white Bengal tiger. The animals are housed in surroundings that closely resemble their natural habitats. Aboard the zoo's air-conditioned monorail, visitors can easily travel from the African plains area, with its herds of antelopes and zebras, to the Australian region, with its ever-popular koalas, kangaroos, and wallabies. A special children's zoo introduces youngsters to many of the zoo's animals, and the Ecology Theater permits a close look at such creatures as an alligator, a rat snake, and an opossum. Located at 12400 S.W. 152 Street in Miami.

② EVERGLADES NATIONAL PARK

The park protects a unique environment, in whch fresh water meets salt water to form one of the rarest and most fragile ecosystems in North America. These shallow waters teem with aquatic life, including alligators and many species of wading birds. Sawgrass plains cover much of the park, and mangroves flourish along the southwestern shore. Approximately 300 different species of birds either live here or make stopovers during migration periods. Bird-watchers are rewarded with close-up views of anhingas, egrets, herons, bald eagles, wood storks, and peregrine falcons. The roseate spoonbill, a once-endangered species, now maintains a stable population here. Boardwalks allow visitors to view the park and its inhabitants on foot. Located 7 miles from Florida City on Hwy. 9336.

③ NAPLES

Located on the Gulf of Mexico, this southwestern coastal town is the gateway to Tamiami Trail and Everglades Parkway (Alligator Alley), the two main routes through Everglades National Park. Most of the town's palm-lined avenues lead to white, sandy beaches. Naples' 1,000-foot pier draws tourists and fishermen alike. This once-quiet fishing town, which got its first traffic light in the mid-1950's, still retains much of its small-town ambience. Aptly named the Village of Venetian Bay, its intricate web of inland water channels is flanked by colonnaded pastel-hued homes. Naples boasts more than a dozen golf courses, and local tennis clubs host several professional tournaments each year. Located on Hwy. 75.

④ CORKSCREW SWAMP SANCTUARY

This 11,000-acre wilderness, operated by the National Audubon Society, lies at the northern tip of Big Cypress Swamp. The sanctuary contains the largest stand of virgin bald cypress trees in North America; core samples indicate that some of these towering trees are more than 700 years old. A 1³/₄-mile-long boardwalk, overhung by Spanish moss, leads visitors through pinelands, wet prairies, and stands of cypress trees. Plants visible along this self-guided trail include hibiscus, ferns, and a variety of orchid species. Cardinals, red-shouldered hawks, and rare birds known as limpkins nest in the sanctuary. Corkscrew Swamp is also the winter home of the nation's largest population of wood storks. Located at exit 17 off Hwy. 75.

⑤ CABBAGE KEY

This tranquil speck of an island, accessible only by boat, has attracted writers and artists to its shores for more than 50 years. The island's only restaurant is wallpapered with thousands of dollar bills—a tradition that began when a fisherman pinned a signed dollar bill to a wall to ensure that he would be able to pay for his next order. Activities on the island include fishing, boating, and walking. From the top of the island's wooden water tower, visitors are rewarded with panoramic views of Pine Island Sound and the Intracoastal Waterway. Located approximately 20 miles northwest of Fort Myers.

⑥ EDISON WINTER HOME

Following the death of his first wife in 1885, Thomas Edison began to spend his winters in Fort Myers. Deciding that he liked the quiet riverfront town, he had a house built to his specifications in Maine and shipped by schooner to Fort Myers, where the pieces were assembled. Today the unpretentious main home, guest house, and laboratory are open to the public. Among several of Edison's innovations in the main house is a lighting system, installed in the 1880's, using handmade light bulbs. Edison's laboratory is filled with test tubes and other apparatus. It was here that the tireless inventor conducted experiments in his quest to produce synthetic rubber. The tropical gardens surrounding the house are lit at night with power supplied by underground wires that Edison installed. The adjoining property was owned by Henry Ford, and the two families wintered together until Edison's death in 1931. The Ford home is also open to the public. Located at 2350 McGregor Blvd. in Fort Myers.

⑦ JOHN AND MABLE RINGLING MUSEUM OF ART

The Ringling Museum complex, a blend of Venetian and Gothic architectural styles, is the legacy of circus impresario John Ringling, the man who ran the "Greatest Show on Earth." Twenty-two galleries display a collection of baroque paintings, tapestries, sculpture, and decorative arts. The central courtyard is dominated by a rare bronze cast of Michelangelo's *David*. The Ringlings' 1920's winter mansion, Cà d'Zan—or "House of John" in Venetian dialect—is a showcase of stained glass, whimsical carvings, and marble terraces. The Circus Museum, located on the grounds of the estate, exhibits posters, photographs, and other memorabilia. Located 4 miles north of Sarasota, off Hwy. 41.

Alligators are among the most prominent inhabitants of Everglades National Park. These reptiles can grow up to 10 feet long.

The tile roofs and fountains of Naples' historic Third Avenue remind many visitors of Italy.

MARK TWAIN'S RIVER

*Savor the moods of the mighty
Mississippi River along the
Great River Road.*

S amuel Langhorne Clemens worked as a Mississippi riverboat pilot from 1857 to 1861, and he came to respect the great river's many moods. He also took his pen name from the call of the crewman who sounded the river's depth as the boat traveled through shallow waters ("Mark twain" means "by the mark two fathoms"). Twain was not the first mortal to commune with the Mississippi, nor was he the last. With a willing ear and just a little imagination, anyone can eavesdrop as it surrenders up its secrets in the soft, gurgling dialect of time.

Below the bluffs at Vicksburg, on a night when moonlight lies on the river like shreds of luminous cloth, one can hear the cannon thunder of a nation at war with itself. Near Greenville, where the cotton rows and bean fields roll away from the delta levees, the sounds of slave auctions are borne by ancient winds. Stare at the face of the water on an idle afternoon and listen to the groan

DAYBREAK

A clump of cypress trees in the Atchafalaya Basin stands silhouetted against a rising sun. Located west of the Mississippi, this wild swampland provides a perfect habitat for alligators, deer, rabbits, and birds.

NOBLE RIVER

Overleaf: Seemingly lifted from the pages of Huckleberry Finn, *a steamboat idles near the landing at Natchez on a placid stretch of the Mississippi River. To the earliest native inhabitants of the region, the river was known as the "Father of Waters."*

of a steamboat chugging toward Memphis, or the first rebellious strains of jazz being played in the canebreaks and cypress bogs down by New Orleans.

What secrets the river holds! It knows Indians and missionaries, pirates and fugitives, planters, trappers, gamblers, lumberjacks, moss pickers, and women of the night. It knows warships and mile-long cargo barges, malaria, mastodons, alligators, carnivorous orchids, and swamp frogs as big as bulldogs. It knows Lewis and Clark and Hernando de Soto, Charles Dickens, William Faulkner, and T. S. Eliot. It knows admiration and condemnation, creation and death.

STEAM-BOATING COUNTRY	This Old Man River is one of the world's great waterways. The fifth-longest river in the world, the Mississippi spreads its arms from the Rockies to

the Alleghenies in a funnel-shaped watershed, collecting the runoff from half the continent—31 states and two Canadian provinces. It courses through time as well as landscape, through American life and culture.

Memphis is an ideal place to begin absorbing the river's geographical scope and rich historical tapestry. Festival Island, linked to downtown by monorail, is the site of the Mud Island Museum that traces 300 years of riverboating. Located outdoors is a realistic, three-dimensional model, 2,600 feet in length, of the Lower Mississippi—from Cairo, Illinois, to New Orleans—complete with flowing water, topographical details, river town depictions, and the region's lore etched in metal plaques. Only an aerial tour could afford visitors such an all-encompassing perspective of a river that is at once reclusive and accessible.

INFORMATION FOR VISITORS

Several steamboat companies offer year-round cruises from Memphis, Tennessee, to New Orleans, Louisiana. Ports of call along the route vary from cruise to cruise. A one-way trip takes approximately eight days. Alternatively, visitors can tour the region by automobile. The Great River Road is composed of several highways that run alongside the river between New Orleans and Memphis. Hwy. 61 is the main route along the eastern bank of the river. A network of smaller roads leads to many plantation mansions, including San Francisco, Houmas House, and Rosedown. Hwy. 65 travels along the western bank, and Hwys. 1 and 18 provide access to Oak Alley and Nottoway Plantations. For more information: Louisiana Office of Tourism, P.O. Box 94291, Baton Rouge, LA 70804-9292. (504) 342-8119.

PADDLE POWER

A giant, steam-powered paddle wheel churns up the Mississippi. Weighing 44 tons, the 18-foot-wide wheel propels the steamboat at a sedate speed of about 8 miles an hour.

44

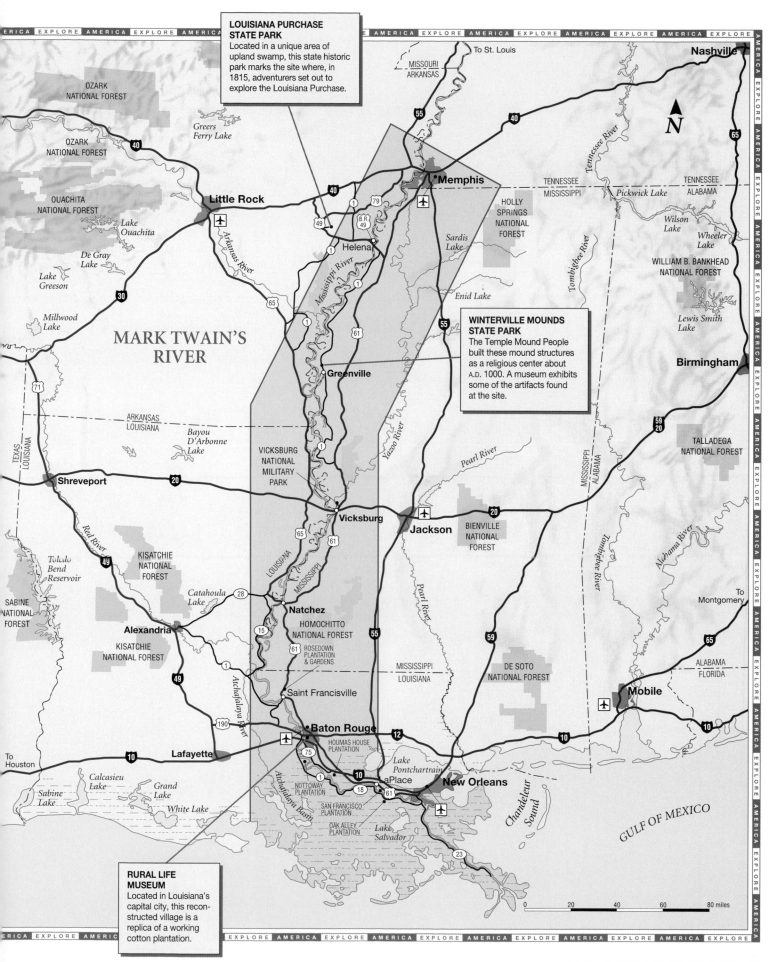

LOUISIANA PURCHASE STATE PARK
Located in a unique area of upland swamp, this state historic park marks the site where, in 1815, adventurers set out to explore the Louisiana Purchase.

WINTERVILLE MOUNDS STATE PARK
The Temple Mound People built these mound structures as a religious center about A.D. 1000. A museum exhibits some of the artifacts found at the site.

RURAL LIFE MUSEUM
Located in Louisiana's capital city, this reconstructed village is a replica of a working cotton plantation.

MARK TWAIN'S RIVER

To St. Louis

Nashville

MISSOURI
ARKANSAS

OZARK NATIONAL FOREST

OZARK NATIONAL FOREST

Greers Ferry Lake

Memphis

TENNESSEE
MISSISSIPPI

TENNESSEE
ALABAMA

Pickwick Lake

OUACHITA NATIONAL FOREST

Little Rock

Lake Ouachita

Helena

HOLLY SPRINGS NATIONAL FOREST

Sardis Lake

Wilson Lake

Wheeler Lake

WILLIAM B. BANKHEAD NATIONAL FOREST

De Gray Lake

Lake Greeson

Arkansas River

Mississippi River

Enid Lake

Tombigbee River

Lewis Smith Lake

Millwood Lake

MARK TWAIN'S RIVER

Greenville

Birmingham

ARKANSAS
LOUISIANA

Bayou D'Arbonne Lake

Yazoo River

Pearl River

TALLADEGA NATIONAL FOREST

TEXAS
LOUISIANA

VICKSBURG NATIONAL MILITARY PARK

MISSISSIPPI
ALABAMA

Shreveport

Red River

Vicksburg

Jackson

BIENVILLE NATIONAL FOREST

Alabama River

KISATCHIE NATIONAL FOREST

Toledo Bend Reservoir

LOUISIANA
MISSISSIPPI

Pearl River

To Montgomery

Catahoula Lake

SABINE NATIONAL FOREST

Natchez

DE SOTO NATIONAL FOREST

Alexandria

HOMOCHITTO NATIONAL FOREST

ROSEDOWN PLANTATION & GARDENS

MISSISSIPPI
LOUISIANA

ALABAMA
FLORIDA

KISATCHIE NATIONAL FOREST

Mobile

Atchafalaya River

Saint Francisville

To Houston

Baton Rouge

HOUMAS HOUSE PLANTATION

Lafayette

Calcasieu Lake

Grand Lake

Atchafalaya Basin

NOTTOWAY PLANTATION

LaPlace

Lake Pontchartrain

New Orleans

Sabine Lake

White Lake

SAN FRANCISCO PLANTATION

Chandeleur Sound

OAK ALLEY PLANTATION

Lake Salvador

GULF OF MEXICO

0   20   40   60   80 miles

From ground level there are two ways to enjoy the Mississippi. One mode is by water: pleasure boats move easily among the swarms of barges and cargo ships laden with grain, ore, manufactured goods, and petroleum products from the American heartland, destined for foreign ports. Several companies operate steam-powered luxury vessels, replicas of the brawny, gaudy cruisers that dominated the river from 1811 to well into the 20th century, when rail became the preferred means of travel.

To a steamboat traveler, the Mississippi seems to run through an endless wilderness. The farms and factories and small towns from Memphis to New Orleans are hidden just beyond levees 30 feet to 60 feet high, which protect the surrounding floodplain from the river's occasional outbreaks. Egrets and herons glide over the water, and nutria laze on logs by the shore.

It is here, from the deck of a paddlewheeler, that one can imagine the river speaking in the language Twain understood, spinning tales of settlers in flatboats battling Indians and yellow fever as they

FROM SHORE TO SHORE
Shrouded in early morning fog, a ferryboat makes its way across the Mississippi to the port of Saint Francisville. The river has always been a major transportation route, carrying passengers and hauling cargo along its 2,340-mile length.

RIVER ROAD PLANTATION
Framed by a canopy of 200-year-old oak trees, Rosedown is just one of the many opulent antebellum homes that line the River Road. The mansion, built in 1835, has a lush 30-acre garden and houses a noteworthy collection of original furniture. During the Civil War, both Confederate and Federal troops were billeted here.

sought high ground; of Farragut's flotilla of gunboats, camouflaged with mud, fighting their way to New Orleans; of steamboat pilots testing the limits of their vessels against the currents.

And it is here, between the levees, that the river reveals its wayward inclinations. From Memphis to Baton Rouge, it twists and turns like discarded twine. The "crookedest river in the world," Mark Twain wrote, "since in one part of its journey it uses up one thousand three hundred miles to cover the same ground that the crow would fly over in six hundred and seventy-five."

THE GREAT RIVER ROAD

Another approach to the Mississippi is by automobile via the Great River Road—a patchwork of federal and state highways, identified by markers bearing a steamboat pilot's wheel—strung along both sides of the river. From this vantage point, too, the river is deceptive. While it dominates life and commerce throughout the lower valley, from outside the levees it is largely invisible and seems separate from the land and its people.

Even those who live nearest to the river are often oblivious to its presence until it tests their ability to contain it, which has happened three times in this century. The levee system, twice as long as the Great Wall of China, began in New Orleans in 1716 and has been extended and strengthened ever since. A ruinous flood in 1927 buried towns and farms and turned hardwood forests into fields of mud. During the flood of 1973, the Mississippi threatened to leave its own channel north of Baton Rouge and join the Atchafalaya River on a shortcut to the Gulf—a calamitous event that would have had immeasurable economic and ecological dimensions. The last catastrophic inundation was in 1993, and no one doubts that more lie ahead.

To explore the Mississippi by automobile is to rummage through the attic of a region that has stored its artifacts carefully. From President's Island—once a colony for freed slaves—south of downtown Memphis, to the marshes below New Orleans, the road is dotted with relics of the river's history and its fables.

From Memphis, the River Road—U.S. Highway 61—peels across the flat, fertile farmland of the Delta, a land that often seems frozen in time. Frequent afternoon rains leave broad, vivid rainbows arcing over deep green fields—a pristine, postcard beauty that masks the harsh reality of life here. Even though the soil is among the richest to be found anywhere, the people are among the poorest in the nation.

For the next 200 miles or so, the river zigzags past a string of oxbow lakes of its own creation and arrives at Vicksburg, one of the most vital Confederate strongholds of the Civil War. From their bluff-top fortress—the "Gibraltar of the Mississippi"—overlooking the river and surrounded by swamps, the 10,000 soldiers of the South controlled an important western trade route. Vicksburg seemed impregnable until Gen. Ulysses S. Grant finally captured the town in April 1863. That bloody slice of history is commemorated in Vicksburg's sprawling National Military Park and Vicksburg National Cemetery, where 17,000 Union soldiers are buried.

Farther downriver is Natchez, where the French established a military outpost in 1714. With more than 500 pre-Civil War buildings still intact, Natchez is the peerless antebellum archive of the lower Mississippi. Dozens of Victorian, Greek Revival, Colonial, and Oriental plantation mansions are opulent reminders of the elegance bought with the tragedy of slavery. At the foot of the bluffs on which the town sits is Natchez-Under-the-Hill, reputed to have been the rowdiest strip of real estate

WHITE GOLD
The fertile soil of the South is perfect for growing cotton, but cleaning the fluffy fibers from the plant's seeds was once a time-consuming process. With the invention of the cotton gin by schoolteacher Eli Whitney in 1793, cotton production soared. Soon many of the planters were wealthy enough to build extravagant homes along the banks of the Mississippi.

on the Mississippi in its day. Saloons, gambling halls, brothels, and other haunts of river riffraff prospered on a mile-long band of lowland that has since been largely washed away. Only a few blocks of Silver Street remain as home to sedate bars and chic restaurants with decks overlooking the river. The most daring action along the riverbank now takes place aboard the *Lady Luck,* a floating casino tethered to land by a sturdy walkway.

The wooded, rolling hills south of Natchez are dotted with tiny towns, historic churches, and antebellum mansions. Noteworthy among the latter are Rosemont, the boyhood home of Jefferson Davis, president of the Confederacy, and Catalpa, a restored Victorian showplace located in an eerie grove of huge live oaks. A couple of miles to the west, the river coils so erratically that in one place it runs nearly due north for several miles before bending southward again and setting a course for Cajun country.

The hills slip gently toward Baton Rouge and then are left behind by the river and the roads that

SOUTHERN COMFORT
Referred to as the White Castle of Louisiana when it was first built, Nottoway plantation hosts one of the largest antebellum homes along the river. This 64-room mansion now operates as a restaurant and inn.

BATTERIES ON THE BLUFFS
Battery Selfridge still stands guard atop the 200-foot bluffs at Vicksburg National Military Park. The artillery overlooked the Mississippi and prevented Union traffic from traveling on the river.

hug its banks. The land becomes flat, and petrochemical plants begin to appear. At night, their lights blaze against the inky sky like oases reassuring river travelers that civilization is close at hand. But by day, they are tangled masses of concrete and metal that crowd up against historic dwellings and intrude on a landscape that grows more primitive as it approaches the Gulf of Mexico.

To the west of the river is the 113-mile-long Atchafalaya River Basin, where black bayous weave through forests of bald cypress trees elegantly draped with Spanish moss. The Acadians, who arrived in Louisiana after being driven out of Nova Scotia in 1755, are the primary inhabitants of the basin. They share it with an assortment of wildlife, including otters and muskrats, alligators and snakes, falcons, pelicans, and 300 other varieties of fowl.

Where the basin makes its steep descent to the coastal marshlands, the Mississippi turns east and heads toward one of the greatest collections of petrochemical plants in the world. Still, this patch of River Road—with its restored mansions of wealthy planters and lumber barons—is one of the state's most popular tourist attractions.

Visitors pick their way past shoulder-to-shoulder factories, seeking out such places as Drestrehan Plantation, the oldest surviving manor on the river, and San Francisco Plantation, perhaps the most spectacular. Woodland Plantation located in LaPlace is the site of the largest and bloodiest slave uprising on record. Here more than 500 slaves revolted, and most were slain by militiamen. Now LaPlace is more happily known for its *andouille*, a spicy Cajun smoked sausage.

For the rest of its journey toward the sea, the Mississippi River is hemmed in by water—Lake Pontchartrain to the left and, to the right, bogs and bayous and smaller lakes and inlets. It enters the heart of New Orleans and curves past warehouses, a grassy pedestrian park, docks, the French Quarter, rail yards, and office towers—reminders of the river's commercial role in American history and its strategic place in westward expansion.

As it heads down a long finger of land that points to its final destination, the mighty Mississippi begins a gentle descent to the Gulf Coast. Cargo vessels ride with it past remote villages that cling to the scarce high ground along the moorlike peninsula, past backwaters where pirates once lay in ambush for merchant ships, past the habitat of giant turtles and sturgeon and migrating eels. Then, in a bird's-foot delta perhaps a hundred miles out, the Mississippi falters and dissipates and is swallowed up by the sea. The river is no more.

GONE FISHING

Fishermen try their luck in the salty water of the Mississippi Delta, where spotted sea trout and redfish thrive.

NEARBY SITES & ATTRACTIONS

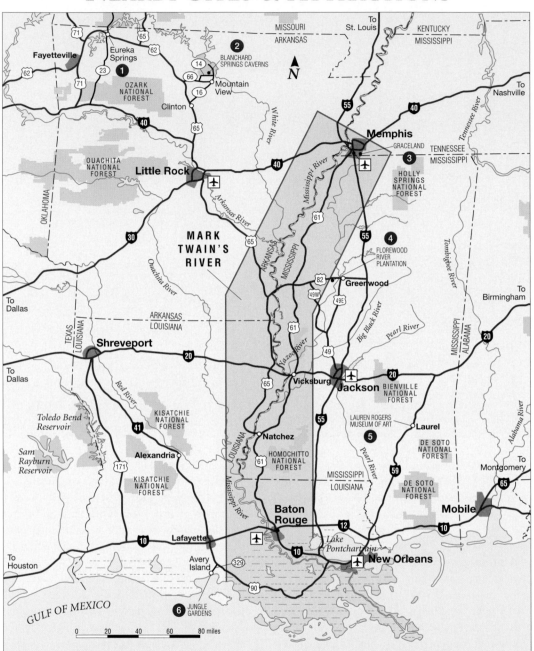

On the grounds of Graceland, Elvis Presley's showcase home in Memphis, the King and his family are buried in the Meditation Garden.

① EUREKA SPRINGS, ARKANSAS

Located in the Ozark Mountains, Eureka Springs is home to several unusual museums. The Frog Fantasies Museum displays clocks, beer steins, and other ornaments, all in the shape of frogs; the Hammond Bell Museum contains more than 1,000 bells, ranging from cow bells to church bells. Another museum exhibits collections of rare Bibles and ancient manuscripts. The town's downtown district is lined with Victorian buildings, the largest collection of such structures in the central United States. The Eureka Springs Trolley takes visitors through the historic district, where they can admire the cupolas, gingerbread trim, and turrets of the town's century-old homes. The Eureka Springs Carnegie Library, financed by industrialist Andrew Carnegie, is another

of these 19th-century treasures. Every spring Eureka Springs hosts the Great Passion Play in its outdoor amphitheater. Located on Hwy. 62 east of Hwy. 23.

② BLANCHARD SPRINGS CAVERNS, ARKANSAS

Located within the Ozark National Forest, Blanchard Springs Caverns has more than seven miles of subterranean rooms and passageways. Guides lead visitors through these underground trails, allowing them to explore the caverns and see stalactites, stalagmites, columns, and flowstones created by the buildup of minerals deposited by dripping water. The 1.2-mile-long Discovery Trail is located in the lower level of the caverns. A paved path leads from one chamber to another, each lit to accent the colorful rock formations. This trail also takes visitors to the origins of the underground spring that flows through the caverns. The Dripstone Trail, which was discovered in 1963, is shorter and less physically demanding than the Discovery Trail. It takes in the enormous Cathedral Room and the Coral Room. Aboveground, the visitor center's audio-visual presentation recounts the geological history of the caverns. Located near Clinton, off Hwy. 14.

3 GRACELAND, TENNESSEE

Once the private home of Elvis Presley, Graceland has been open to the public since 1982. Elvis lived here for 20 years, and guided tours of the house provide visitors with a glimpse of his lifestyle. The wrought-iron gates to the 20,000-square-foot, white-columned mansion are decorated with musical notes and the figure of a musician playing a guitar. The living room, complete with a 15-foot-long white sofa, and the pool room, decorated as an old-fashioned billiard parlor, are included on the tour. The Trophy Room, housed in a separate building, displays Elvis's army uniform, a collection of his first Sun Studio records, and the largest private collection of gold records in the world, including his first gold single, "Heartbreak Hotel." Another museum across the street is devoted to Elvis's automobile, motorcycle, and private jet collections. A 1955 pink Fleetwood Cadillac and a customized Convair 880 jet with 24-karat gold seat-belt buckles are also on display. Located at 3747 Elvis Presley Blvd. in Memphis.

4 FLOREWOOD RIVER PLANTATION, MISSISSIPPI

This reconstructed 1850's plantation illustrates the history of the cotton industry. Located on 100 acres of land near the Yazoo River, the museum includes the planter's elegantly furnished mansion, a number of outbuildings, and the plantation grounds. A well-restored box-bed Lane and Bodley steam engine and a hand-operated Whitney cotton gin are also on display. Costumed interpreters greet visitors to the mansion. A tour of the house includes the dining room and the master bedroom, furnished with a wig-dresser, a petticoat table, and the bedroom furniture of Confederate general Nathan Bedford Forrest. Some of the outbuildings offer live demonstrations, including the cookhouse, carriage house, blacksmith shop, and the gin building, where cotton was prepared and baled for transportation. Approximately three acres of cotton are still planted here. In the fall visitors are welcome to help pick the cotton. Live oak, peach, southern wax myrtle, and Callery pear are just a few of the different species of trees that thrive on the grounds. Located west of Greenwood on Hwy. 82.

5 LAUREN ROGERS MUSEUM OF ART, MISSISSIPPI

This museum, considered to be one of the finest in the South, houses an extensive collection of 19th- and 20th-century international and American paintings, etchings, and craftwork. American Impressionist and Hudson River School works dominate the collection. Landscape paintings include works by James McNeill Whistler and Winslow Homer, as well as Thomas Moran's *Sunset, Long Island Sound*. The museum also contains several of Albert Bierstadt's American wilderness paintings, and works by portrait painter John Singer Sargent. A fine collection of Georgian silverware is on display, including a 1770 tea urn that belonged to George III, cake baskets, and the plates of England's preeminent silversmith of the 18th century, Paul Lamerie. Also on display is an extensive collection of baskets, which demonstrates the skills of some of the major Indian nations of North America. Highlighting the collection are the rare feathered baskets created by the Pomo Indians of the California basin region. Another wing of the museum displays 18th- and 19th-century Japanese woodblock prints. Located in the downtown historic district of Laurel.

6 JUNGLE GARDENS OF AVERY ISLAND, LOUISIANA

Jungle Gardens covers an area equal to 36 city blocks and houses an eclectic variety of plants from all corners of the globe. There are finger bananas from China, papyrus and lotus from Egypt, Chinese wisterias that are grown as trees, and 60-foot canes of Chinese timber bamboo. The gardens provide a fertile environment for a variety of plants from India, including magnolias, crepe myrtles, junipers, and soap trees. Azaleas and camellias carpet great expanses of the gardens. Numerous walking trails and roads make these botanical treasures easily accessible to visitors. Established in 1936 by Edward McIlhenny, the gardens also protect a number of endangered bird species, including 20,000 herons and egrets, which congregate in an area known as Bird City. Located on Hwy. 329 just off Hwy. 90.

This woven straw water bottle, on display in the Lauren Rogers Museum of Art, was found in Chaco Canyon, New Mexico. The bottle was made by Pueblo Indians in approximately A.D. 1150. The inside of the bottle was sealed with pitch to make it waterproof.

The Jungle Gardens of Avery Island provide a refuge for white-tailed deer, seen here amid a profusion of blossoming azaleas.

THE OREGON TRAIL

Stretching across six states, this historic trail still reverberates with the dreams of the earliest immigrants.

They walked by the thousands. Beginning in 1841, over the course of 20 years between 300,000 and 350,000 pioneers marched from Independence, Missouri, to the Willamette Valley, some 2,170 miles away in Oregon. Their odyssey took seed in the most compelling of human urges—the search for a fresh start. It was fueled by the most irresistible of all human impulses—the surge of hope over experience. No matter how arduous the journey, how high the price, the pioneers took one grueling step after another. This is the story of the Oregon Trail.

This teeming mass of men, women and children, blacksmiths, tinkers, tailors, and preachers did not have to be told they were marching into history. From the moment they left Missouri, many seemed to sense that they were engaged in an adventure that would not soon be forgotten. Thousands of them recorded the heartaches, the terrors, and the splendors of their arduous journey westward; more than 3,000 of these pioneer diaries have been found and excerpts published.

The stories that leap from their pages are as engaging as any novel.

In Missouri and Kansas, in Nebraska, Wyoming, and Idaho, visitors can still walk in the ruts etched deep into the landscape by the passing of tens of thousands of heavily laden wagons. From start to finish, it would take at least two weeks to follow the entire Oregon Trail. A more feasible approach would be to concentrate on the choicest segment and last leg of the trail, beginning in Farewell Bend, Oregon, where the Snake River heads north into Hells Canyon.

RIVERS AND CANYONS

One hundred fifty years after the great trek, Oregon's landscape remains virtually unchanged. Here are seamless deserts, where the air is heavy with silence and the scent of sage. Here are rivers that surge through canyons carved by tempest and polished by time. Here are soaring, snowcapped summits reaching for the sky. Here are clouds, roaring in from the Pacific, rebounding off volcanic peaks to crash back upon forests full of firs that were already ancient the day Columbus landed. It was at their campsite at Farewell Bend that emigrants bade farewell to Idaho and to the Snake River. The cauldron of Hells Canyon presented an impenetrable barrier, so for the final leg of their journey the pioneers turned their wagons west and commenced the rigorous climb to the Columbia Plateau.

Suddenly the struggle intensified. An early fall snowstorm in the Blue Mountains invariably reminded wagon trains that the journey now was a race—a sprint against the seasons. For soon they would see, glistening on the horizon, the final portals to paradise—the towering Cascades. Once winter storms settled upon these peaks and passes, all hope of reaching the trail's end would be dashed.

The pioneers' unsprung wagons were far too uncomfortable to ride, so most people walked. Before they were through, more than 10 percent of them—men, women, and children—lay in trailside graves. Abigail Jane Scott wrote this poignant entry in her journal in 1852: "Made twenty miles; we passed eight fresh graves." The typical pioneer wagon was small—its hard hickory bed measured 10 feet long by 4 feet wide, with sideboards 2 feet high. The canvas top might be gaily painted with the slogan: "Oregon or Bust." Into this wagon, drawn by six or eight oxen, a family crammed a ton of dreams.

In the shadow of the Wallowa Mountains, less than an hour's drive from Farewell Bend, stands Flagstaff Hill. From this lofty perch, the pioneers gazed down upon Lone Pine Valley, a green oasis that offered the first hint of all the bounty that

WAGON RELICS
Rusted wagon parts are a reminder of the hardships of the journey. Fall rains turned the trail to a deep sea of mud. Many pioneers were forced to abandon their wagons and all but a handful of belongings before it was rendered impassable by the first winter snow.

THE PROMISED LAND
Overleaf: The Willamette Valley, at the end of the Oregon Trail, is a glorious land of rolling wheat fields.

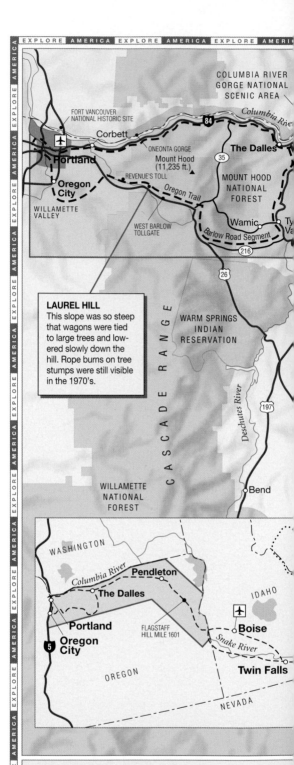

LAUREL HILL
This slope was so steep that wagons were tied to large trees and lowered slowly down the hill. Rope burns on tree stumps were still visible in the 1970's.

WAGONS WEST
Travelers can relive the pioneer experience on a covered wagon trip along sections of the Oregon Trail. Companies offering tours include CJ Lodge Covered Wagon & Horse Rides, P.O. Box 130, Maupin, OR 97037, (503) 395-2404; Wagons West Ltd., 31 NW Thatcher Rd., Forest Grove, OR 97116, (503) 357-5757; Oregon Trail Trolley, Rte. 1, Box 15, Haines, OR 97833, (503) 856-3356.

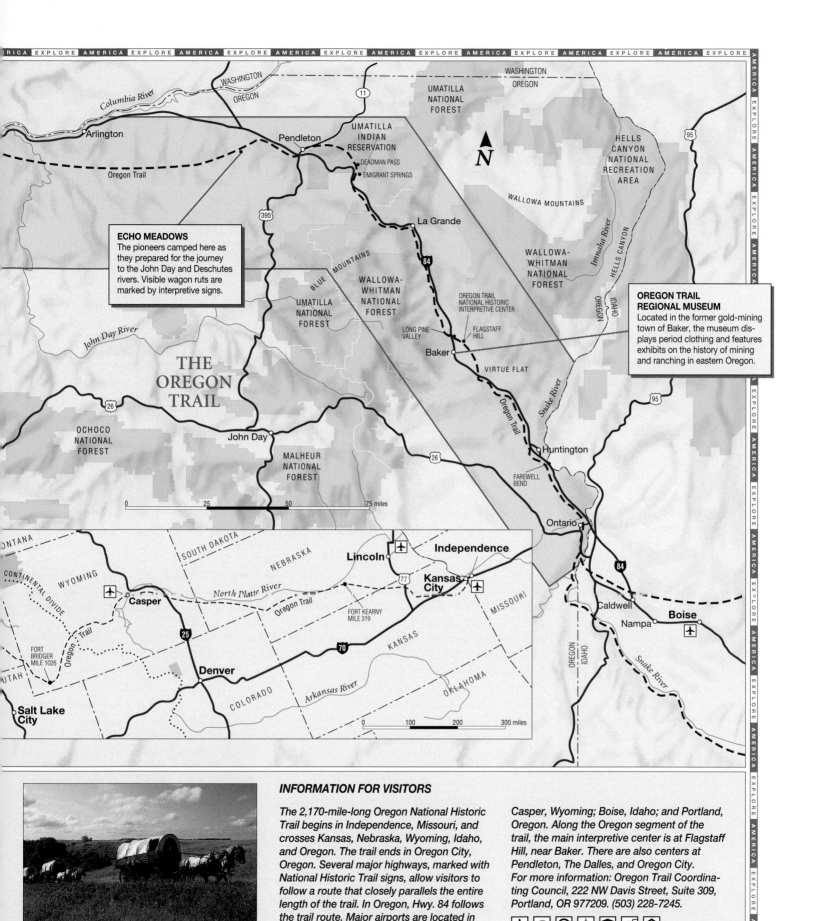

ECHO MEADOWS
The pioneers camped here as they prepared for the journey to the John Day and Deschutes rivers. Visible wagon ruts are marked by interpretive signs.

OREGON TRAIL REGIONAL MUSEUM
Located in the former gold-mining town of Baker, the museum displays period clothing and features exhibits on the history of mining and ranching in eastern Oregon.

THE OREGON TRAIL

INFORMATION FOR VISITORS

The 2,170-mile-long Oregon National Historic Trail begins in Independence, Missouri, and crosses Kansas, Nebraska, Wyoming, Idaho, and Oregon. The trail ends in Oregon City, Oregon. Several major highways, marked with National Historic Trail signs, allow visitors to follow a route that closely parallels the entire length of the trail. In Oregon, Hwy. 84 follows the trail route. Major airports are located in Kansas City, Kansas; Lincoln, Nebraska; Casper, Wyoming; Boise, Idaho; and Portland, Oregon. Along the Oregon segment of the trail, the main interpretive center is at Flagstaff Hill, near Baker. There are also centers at Pendleton, The Dalles, and Oregon City. For more information: Oregon Trail Coordinating Council, 222 NW Davis Street, Suite 309, Portland, OR 977209. (503) 228-7245.

Once a welcome halt for trekkers, the Umatilla Valley town of Pendleton boomed in the 1860's when grain and woolen industries were established in this corner of northeastern Oregon. The town still retains the flavor of the Old West and hosts an annual rodeo—the Pendleton Roundup—for four days each September.

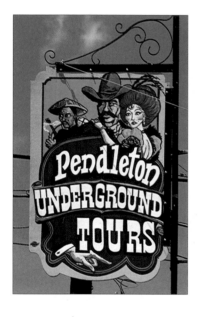

PENDLETON'S PAST

Tours of Pendleton Underground open up the network of hand-dug tunnels that connected the bars, brothels, and gambling dens of pioneer-era Pendleton. The tunnels were also used by Chinese railroad laborers to get to their living quarters and businesses, as well as to avoid the anti-Chinese feelings of the town's white citizens.

Oregon had in store. They gazed back, too, across Virtue Flat, an almost unbroken bed of tumbleweed and sagebrush.

Flagstaff Hill is now home to the National Historic Oregon Trail Interpretive Center, where children can load up a real wagon, and interactive exhibits and living-history demonstrations plunge visitors into the details of pioneer life. Modern-day travelers may walk alongside ruts left by the wagon trains a century and a half ago. These parallel wagon ruts are among the most celebrated of the entire Oregon Trail.

From this summit in 1843, an observer would not have seen the smoke of a single fire. Ten years later, settlements had mushroomed around a string of trading posts, bridges, forts, and stagecoach stations. By 1855 there was a steady stream of east-west traffic on the trail.

About an hour-and-a-half drive west of Baker City, the Oregon Trail crosses the Umatilla Indian Reservation. Here the Umatillas, along with the

Walla Walla and the Cayuse, are engaged in a pioneering effort of their own. In 1995 they began work on a unique interpretive center that will tell the story of the Oregon Trail from the perspective of those who lived on this land before the coming of the pioneers. The Umatilla center will serve as a salient reminder that, in the 1840's, the first immigrants were welcomed by Native American tribes, who gladly offered help to the newcomers. Indeed, few pioneers would have survived the rigors of the trail without Indian assistance in tracking game and fording rivers. It was not until the 1860's that relations soured between settlers and natives.

In the cowboy town of Pendleton, 90 minutes west of Baker City, the sidewalks are scuffed by spurs and the air is filled with the scent of saddle and sage. Hamley's, one of the West's legendary saddleries, still welcomes visitors. At the shop, craftsmen cut and shape the coveted seats of both local ranchers and national rodeo champions. No tour of Pendleton is complete without a visit to its

BARLOW ROAD
To avoid the Columbia River, wagon companies blazed a trail in 1846 from The Dalles across the Cascade Mountains. This overland route, known as the Barlow Road, unfortunately proved every bit as dangerous as the great river—and almost as wet. A replica of the West Barlow Tollgate, left, marks where the last tollgate stood on the Barlow Road.

RIVER CROSSING
Wreaths of mist drift over the Sandy River, below, on the old Barlow Road Route. When settler Francis Revenue built a bridge across the river, pioneers had to pay him a toll before they could cross.

an ox bought in Missouri for $30 could be sold in Portland for $120. A $100 horse could fetch $500. Most profitable were milking cows. A $12 heifer might be worth $150 by the time she reached the Willamette Valley.

<table>
<tr><td>A FORK IN
THE ROAD</td></tr>
</table>

A FORK IN THE ROAD   About 125 miles west of Pendleton, the trail reaches the riverfront town of The Dalles, gateway to the Columbia River Gorge, a national scenic area. Here, the mighty Columbia carves through the Cascades in a head-long rush from heartland to sea. At this point the pioneers were forced to pause, and then to pray.

Wrapped in mist, lashed by wind, and chilled by shadow, the narrow gorge forced early immigrants to abandon overland travel and take to the great river of the West. They took apart their wagons, lashed them upon makeshift rafts or to the vessels of hired Indian boatmen, and floated into the jaws of this terrifying chasm.

The Columbia, now tamed by dams upstream that create a chain of quiescent pools was once a

VERDANT SPLENDOR
Shade-loving plants cloak the walls of Oneonta Gorge, above, close to the Columbia River.

celebrated bordello. Nowadays the working girls are mannequins attired in period finery.

As the trail continues west, the names of the towns, creeks, and roadside rest areas—from the sylvan calm of Emigrant Springs to the raw peril of Deadman's Pass—hark back to the pioneers' arduous passage. As dawn's trumpet blasted over the horizon, pioneers scurried to round up live-stock that might have wandered miles in search of fresh grazing. Families walked all morning, rested, walked again until dark, ate another meal of bacon and beans, and fell asleep again underneath the wagon. On some evenings, an old man played the fiddle or a young girl sang a hymn. And so it went, day after endless 20-mile, dust-caked day.

Pioneers who took care of their livestock could profit considerably at the end of the trail. In 1852,

cacophony of rushing rapids. The downstream journey, with winds working against the current, was both prolonged and perilous. As the immigrants passed beneath soaring basalt cliffs—cloaked in lichen, etched by time—some sang hymns. Some were still singing as they drowned.

Today visitors can drive the spectacular riverside freeway as far as Corbett, marveling at the tumbling waterfalls along the way. Then, after following the stretch of the pioneer trail that runs along the Columbia River, they may backtrack 40 miles to The Dalles and take the Barlow Road through the Tygh Valley and the town of Wamic on a well-marked, 100-mile scenic drive all the way around majestic Mount Hood.

The immigrants who finally arrived in the Willamette Valley still had many hardships ahead of them. These travel-weary settlers had to erect shelters and begin farming the fertile land. They were starting from scratch—building a new life in an untamed land. They came to change the land, but found instead that the land changed them. It made them Oregonians.

ONE-STOP SHOPPING
Fort Vancouver National Historic Site, outside Portland, preserves the British fur-trading post that greeted the new arrivals at the western end of the Oregon Trail. It was here that Dr. John McLoughlin, chief factor of the Hudson's Bay Company, welcomed the exhausted settlers and provisioned them with seed, lumber, and cattle, all on credit.

JOURNEY'S END
Snowcapped Mount Hood, at an elevation of 11,235 feet, was a sign to the pioneers that their final destination was close at hand.

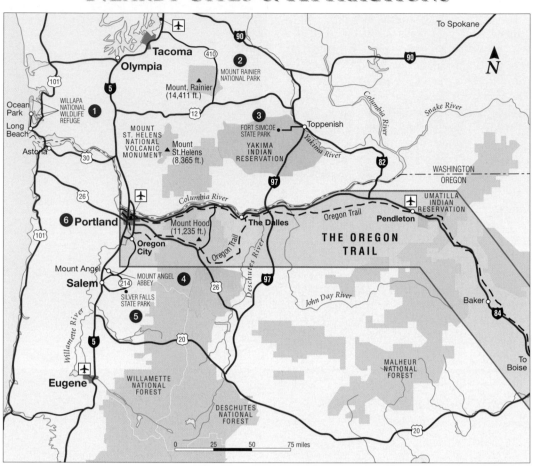

A modern symbol of the city of Portland, the six-ton, hammered-copper statue Portlandia *perches proudly on a pedestal in front of the Portland Building.*

① WILLAPA NATIONAL WILDLIFE REFUGE, WASHINGTON

Established in 1937, the refuge protects a diverse seascape of sand dunes, mud flats, salt marshes, and intertidal pools. Clams, crabs, oysters, fish, and other marine life thrive in the nutrient-rich waters of the bay, fed by the waters of the Pacific Ocean and by the many small rivers that flow into Willapa Bay. Thousands of shorebirds and waterfowl feed and rest in the refuge during their spring and fall migration periods. At different times of the year, bird-watchers can spot Canada geese, canvasback ducks, loons, bald eagles, herons, and cormorants. Beds of eel-grass that grow in the intertidal zones bring the black brant to the refuge during its annual flight between Alaska and Mexico. The coastal forest of Long Island provides an ideal habitat for deer, elks, and bears. The refuge headquarters is located near milepost 24 on Hwy. 101.

② MOUNT RAINIER NATIONAL PARK, WASHINGTON

At an elevation of 14,411 feet, Mount Rainier ranks as the fifth-highest peak in the United States and is the star attraction within the park's 235,612 acres of forests, alpine meadows, and glaciers. Eighty miles of paved roads that are open from late May through mid-October allow visitors to enjoy this rugged scenery. The most popular road trip is a 13-mile route that is open year-round and climbs to a 5,557-foot alpine meadow known as Paradise, which is carpeted in summer with a profusion of wildflowers. Zigzagging through the park are 240 miles of hiking trails, including the challenging 93-mile-long Wonderland Trail. The Mount Rainier Scenic Railroad offers visitors a less strenuous way of soaking up the scenery. During the winter months, the park is popular with cross-country skiers. Located 74 miles southeast of Tacoma.

③ FORT SIMCOE STATE PARK, WASHINGTON

Built in 1856, Fort Simcoe helped to avert the threat of hostilities between the local Yakima Indians and white settlers and miners flocking to the region. Relations improved by 1859, and the fort served for the next 60 years as an Indian Agency headquarters. Of Fort Simcoe's original 35 buildings, only five still stand, including the captains' dwellings, a squared-log blockhouse, and the commander's house, which has been restored and furnished as it had been in the late 1850's. Visitors may also tour the reconstructed log barracks and blockhouses. A small museum recounts the history of the fort and the Yakima Indians. Located 27 miles from the town of Toppenish on Hwy. 220.

④ MOUNT ANGEL ABBEY, OREGON

In 1882 a group of Benedictine monks relocated to Oregon from their 800-year-old abbey in the Swiss Alps. Here they founded Mount Angel Abbey, and in the spirit of their patron, Saint Benedict, they turned to farming and opened a school. Today there are 100 members of the religious community, and certain parts of the monastery are open to visitors. Of particular interest are a state-of-the-art library, which houses a collection of ancient manuscripts, as well as a newly renovated museum with an eclectic collection. The abbey also has a guest house for those seeking a quiet place for reflection and prayer. Located northeast of Salem on Hwy. 214.

⑤ SILVER FALLS STATE PARK, OREGON

Named for its shimmering waterfalls, Oregon's largest state park was established in 1931. Located in the western foothills of the Cascade Mountains, the park's 8,700 acres are forested with Douglas fir, western hemlock, and western red cedar. Maple, alder, and cottonwood trees carpet the lower elevations. Visitors can view the park's 10 waterfalls along the seven-mile Trail of Ten Falls. The highest among them, South Falls, cascades 177 feet into Silver Creek Canyon. In addition, the park offers miles of jogging, bicycling, and equestrian trails. Located 26 miles east of Salem on Hwy. 214.

⑥ PORTLAND, OREGON

Compact, manageable, and human-scaled, this city of 1.7 million people, situated on the Willamette River, well deserves its reputation as one of the most livable cities in the United States. Portland's city center is rich in carefully restored buildings; the Old Town Historic District, the site of the city's first settlement in 1844, contains one of the nation's largest collections of cast-iron buildings. A few blocks south of the historic district is Portland's downtown core. Here, the colorful Portland Building—the nation's first postmodern public building, designed by the renowned architect Michael Graves—serves as a backdrop for the statue of *Portlandia*, the largest hammered-copper sculpture commissioned since the Statue of Liberty. Portland's temperate climate keeps the city's 200 parks green year-round. Washington Park is home to the International Rose Test Garden, which displays 400 varieties of roses, as well as the Japanese Gardens—a haven of serenity in the midst of its urban surroundings. In the city's northwest corner, Forest Park—one of the largest city parks in the nation—stretches for several miles and is a haven for wildlife. The Portland Art Museum boasts a renowned collection of Northwest Coast Indian artifacts. Visitors to the Oregon Museum of Science and Industry can tour the interior of the U.S.S. *Blueback*, a diesel-and-electric-powered submarine that remained in service for 31 years.

The gardens of Mount Angel Abbey form a colorful counterpoint to the ecclesiastical architecture of this hilltop Benedictine monastery.

Fields of delicate wildflowers offset the jagged snowcapped peaks of the Tatoosh Mountains in Mount Rainier National Park.

RAFTING THE COLORADO RIVER

*The majesty of the Grand Canyon
provides a spectacular backdrop for this
exciting journey of a lifetime.*

Sunlit cliffs tower overhead, and the liquid notes of a canyon wren spill off the walls. The river ripples softly, and the branches of trees on shore dance in a gentle breeze. Violet-green swallows swoop down in an iridescent flash, snatching insects from the air. Ravens squawk and gurgle as they slowly wheel alongside the ever-rising walls of the canyon. All thoughts of the outside world vanish as the Colorado River and its grandest canyon play their music. Such moments, when time hangs suspended, are one of the greatest pleasures of traveling by boat down the river through the Grand Canyon.

This is a journey along one of the longest stretches of wild river left in the United States—through the 1-million-acre Grand Canyon National Park. Although many visitors choose to experience the grandeur of the Grand Canyon from lookout points on the North and South rims, more adventurous souls opt for a view from the canyon bottom. Surrounded by steep canyon walls—in places a mile high—that were etched into the Colorado Plateau by the force of moving water during a period of more than 5 million years, boaters come to respect the river and its role as the creator of one of the most magnificent landscapes on the planet.

River trips begin at Lees Ferry, just below Glen Canyon Dam in far northern Arizona. From Lees Ferry, at mile zero, to the first disembarkation point at Diamond Creek, the distance is 226 miles. Other than by boat, the only way in or out is on foot. Once the boats are carefully loaded and passengers are issued orange life jackets, it's time to board. With little fanfare the boats pull gently into the waiting embrace of the Colorado River.

After passing under Navajo Bridge—almost the only sign of civilization until

Phantom Ranch—the boats enter Marble Canyon. This southern stretch of the Grand Canyon was named by Maj. John Wesley Powell, who observed, "The limestone of this canyon is often polished, and makes a beautiful marble." The limestone has not actually been changed to marble, but it does have that appearance.

THE FIRST
EXPLORER

John Wesley Powell is synonymous with the Colorado River and the Grand Canyon. At age 35, fresh out of army service during the Civil War, he became a geologist and decided to navigate two of the great rivers of the West—the Green and the Colorado. He is credited as the first to do so. Powell set out from Green River, Wyoming, on May 24, 1869, and by mid-August was at the portal to the Grand Canyon.

He and his crew had started with four wooden boats, three of oak and one of pine. Two weeks into the expedition, one had been smashed to smithereens in a rock-strewn rapid. As they made their way through the Grand Canyon, they frequently were forced to portage the remaining boats over treacherous shores. Powell, who'd lost an arm in a Civil War battle, toiled alongside his men and scrambled up sheer cliffs with no apparent regard for his physical limitation.

By the time Powell and his men were halfway through the canyon, their 10 months' worth of rations were sorely depleted—some rancid bacon, soggy flour, and a little coffee was about all they had left. Unaware that they were almost out of the canyon, three disgruntled crewmen hiked out to the plateau and lost their lives.

But to the indefatigable and ever-optimistic Powell, the Grand Canyon was "a land of song. Mountains of music swell in the rivers, hills of music billow in the creeks, and meadows of music murmur in the rills that ripple over the rocks. Altogether it is a symphony of multitudinous melodies. All this is the music of waters."

Beyond the thin green strip of the immediate river corridor, the Grand Canyon is a pure desert of spiny cactus and small gray-green shrubs. The water temperature, a cool 48° to 50°F as it flows fresh from the depths of Lake Powell upstream, provides delightful relief from the heat. So do dramatic summer thunderstorms, which can send waterfalls cascading down dry cliffs and turn the Colorado River back to its old silt-thick, rusty hue.

Each night boaters pitch tents on broad, sandy beaches. After dinner the air cools, the river laps lazily at the shore, and bats flutter in the gathering dusk like leaves blowing in the wind. Lingering sunlight burnishes the rimrock with a band of gold. The evening's entertainment consists of simply

OAR POWER
A row of brightly colored dories, pulled up on a sandy beach, awaits the next day's adventure. These narrow, high-sided boats allow present-day adventurers to retrace Major Powell's 1869 voyage.

A RIVER'S CANYON
Overleaf: A placid stretch of the Colorado River meanders through Conquistador Aisle. Gigantic boulders, once part of the canyon walls, have been carried away by the river and stockpiled at the mouths of the side canyons.

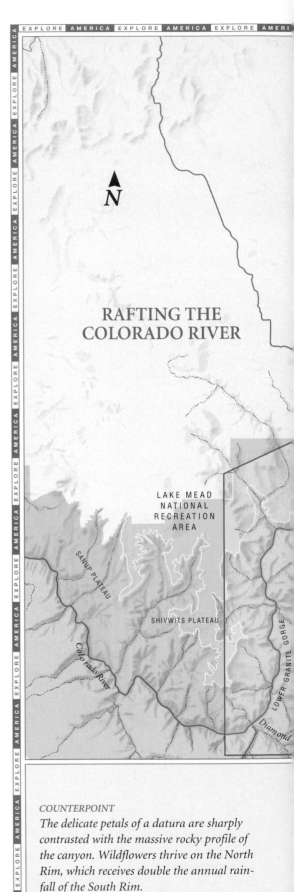

RAFTING THE
COLORADO RIVER

LAKE MEAD
NATIONAL
RECREATION
AREA

SANUP PLATEAU

SHIVWITS PLATEAU

Colorado River

LOWER GRANITE GORGE

Diamond

COUNTERPOINT
The delicate petals of a datura are sharply contrasted with the massive rocky profile of the canyon. Wildflowers thrive on the North Rim, which receives double the annual rainfall of the South Rim.

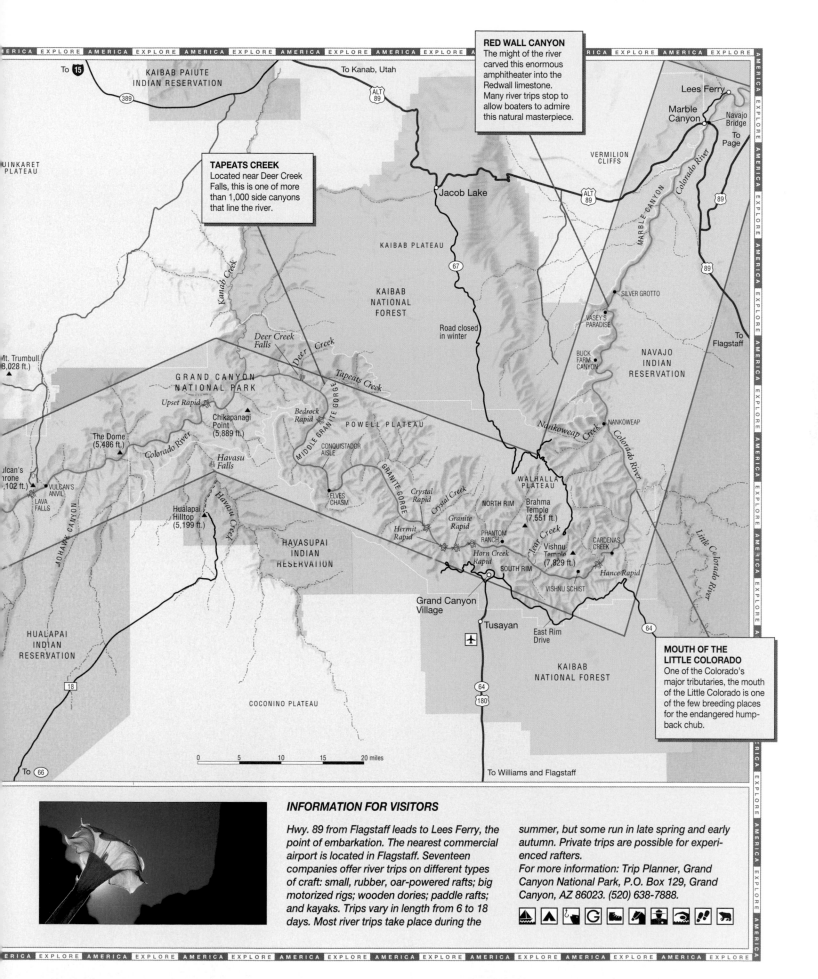

RED WALL CANYON
The might of the river carved this enormous amphitheater into the Redwall limestone. Many river trips stop to allow boaters to admire this natural masterpiece.

TAPEATS CREEK
Located near Deer Creek Falls, this is one of more than 1,000 side canyons that line the river.

MOUTH OF THE LITTLE COLORADO
One of the Colorado's major tributaries, the mouth of the Little Colorado is one of the few breeding places for the endangered humpback chub.

KAIBAB PAIUTE
INDIAN RESERVATION

To 15
389
To Kanab, Utah
ALT 89

Lees Ferry
Marble Canyon
Navajo Bridge
To Page
89

VERMILION CLIFFS

UINKARET PLATEAU

Jacob Lake

ALT 89

To Flagstaff

KAIBAB PLATEAU

67

KAIBAB NATIONAL FOREST

Road closed in winter

SILVER GROTTO

VASEY'S PARADISE

BUCK FARM CANYON

NAVAJO INDIAN RESERVATION

Kanab Creek

Deer Creek Falls
Deer Creek
Tapeats Creek

Mt. Trumbull
(8,028 ft.)

GRAND CANYON NATIONAL PARK

Upset Rapid
Chikapanagi Point (5,889 ft.)
Bedrock Rapid
MIDDLE GRANITE GORGE
POWELL PLATEAU

Nankoweap Creek
NANKOWEAP
Colorado River

The Dome (5,486 ft.)
Colorado River
Havasu Falls

CONQUISTADOR AISLE

WALHALLA PLATEAU

Vulcan's Throne (3,102 ft.)
VULCAN'S ANVIL
LAVA FALLS

ELVES CHASM

GRANITE GORGE

Crystal Rapid
Crystal Creek
NORTH RIM
Brahma Temple (7,551 ft.)

Little Colorado River

Hualapai Hilltop (5,199 ft.)
Havasu Creek

HAVASUPAI INDIAN RESERVATION

Hermit Rapid
Granite Rapid
PHANTOM RANCH

Horn Creek Rapid
SOUTH RIM

Clear Creek
Vishnu Temple (7,829 ft.)
CARDENAS CREEK

Hance Rapid

JOHAWK CANYON

VISHNU SCHIST

HUALAPAI INDIAN RESERVATION

Grand Canyon Village

18

Tusayan

64

East Rim Drive

COCONINO PLATEAU

64
180

KAIBAB NATIONAL FOREST

To 66

0 5 10 15 20 miles

To Williams and Flagstaff

INFORMATION FOR VISITORS

Hwy. 89 from Flagstaff leads to Lees Ferry, the point of embarkation. The nearest commercial airport is located in Flagstaff. Seventeen companies offer river trips on different types of craft: small, rubber, oar-powered rafts; big motorized rigs; wooden dories; paddle rafts; and kayaks. Trips vary in length from 6 to 18 days. Most river trips take place during the summer, *but some run in late spring and early autumn. Private trips are possible for experienced rafters.*

For more information: Trip Planner, Grand Canyon National Park, P.O. Box 129, Grand Canyon, AZ 86023. (520) 638-7888.

watching stars crystallize in the darkening sky and discussing the day's journey.

Mile by mile the Colorado River dives deeper into the earth and into time. Below swashbuckling Hance Rapid, the boats enter the narrow confines of the Inner Gorge. Here, heat waves shimmer off the shiny black Vishnu Schist, rock that is almost 2 billion years old. Spiky agaves and rotund barrel cactus cling to clefts in the tortured schist. Atop the Vishnu another 5,000 feet of rock is stacked up to the rims of the canyon, presenting one of the most complete displays of geologic history on earth.

Each day in the Grand Canyon brings countless opportunities for exploration and discoveries: on hikes up side canyons such as Buck Farm, a tiny canyon tree frog is seen huddling on a boulder. A steep trail above Nankoweap leads to the stone gra-

naries where Anasazi Indians stored their corn 1,000 years ago. Nankoweap is one of about 2,700 archeological sites recorded in Grand Canyon National Park, revealing human habitation in and around the canyon for at least the past 4,000 years.

There's Vasey's Paradise, a magnificent oasis, named by John Wesley Powell for his botanist friend. The clear, perennial springs that burst from Redwall limestone support hanging gardens of golden columbines, crimson monkeyflowers, and emerald maidenhair ferns. A walk up Clear Creek leads to a waterfall behind which an American dipper erects its nest. These and many other spots are special places, each part of the magnificent ensemble that is the Grand Canyon.

But for many people, the adrenaline-rushing thrill of riding the rapids is the reason they make

WHITE-WATER MASTERY

An experienced guide skillfully maneuvers a motorized raft through Hermit Rapid. Although the average velocity of the river is about four miles an hour, it surges through rapids at nearly twice that speed. The Colorado drops 2,000 feet on its 277-mile run through the canyon.

this journey. The hundred or so rapids on the Colorado River in the Grand Canyon are formed by boulders that have washed in from side canyons. The boulders present obstacles to the river, which either goes over, under, or around. When the flow is great enough, the river will rearrange and sweep away those boulders. It's a constant contest between the river and its tributaries: one giving, the other taking away.

The names of the big rapids assume greater meaning as boats accelerate into a frenzy of furious, slamming, soaking waves: Hance, Horn, Hermit, Granite, Bedrock, Upset. Although some runs are over in an instant, novice boaters quickly gain an inkling of just what this river can do, how fast it can move, what force it holds.

Two rapids stand out—their names spoken with admiration and trepidation by experienced Grand Canyon boaters: Crystal and Lava Falls. Crystal Rapid, at mile 98, was inconsequential until December 3, 1966. That night, and during the next three days, a winter storm dumped 14 inches of

ANCIENT SCULPTURES
Powerful currents have exposed, shaped, and polished the hard Vishnu schist into fluted master-pieces, above left. The schist, located 4,000 feet below the North Rim, is the oldest rock in the region. Elves Chasm, above, is a paradise of sparkling waterfalls and crystal-clear pools, where maidenhair ferns and mosses cling to the rock face.

rain on the North Rim of the canyon. A slurry of boulders, silt, sand, and water roared down Crystal Creek, installing house-size rocks in the river channel and forcing most of the current against the left wall. The centerpiece of Crystal is now a giant boat-eating "hole" formed by water flowing over a huge boulder near the left bank. Successful navigation at most water levels usually demands a far-right run. To keep things interesting, a bumpy rock garden lurks in the lower reaches of the rapid that nobody wants to swim.

Water level, measured in cubic feet per second and governed by daily releases upstream at Glen Canyon Dam, dictates the difficulty of a run. Some rapids get easier at high water, others get harder. On

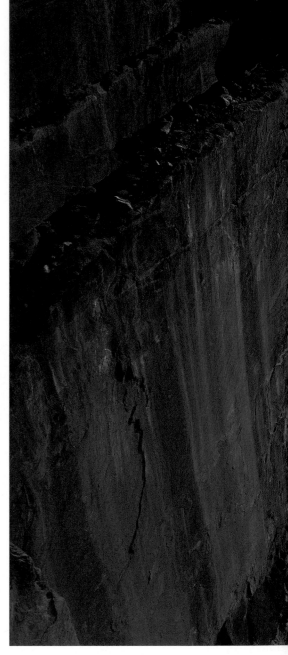

ANASAZI RUINS

Hilltop ruins near Cardenas Creek are part of the legacy of the Anasazi, who inhabited the Grand Canyon about 2,000 years ago. The ruins were discovered in 1890 by Robert Brewster Stanton, whose dream was to build a railroad through the canyon.

the standard scale by which rapids are rated on western rivers, 10 is the highest number a rapid can receive in terms of degree of difficulty. In the guidebooks, Crystal always rates a 9 or 10. At extremely high water levels, Crystal is so risky that some river parties choose to wait until the water drops and the passage can be made with less risk.

RUNNING LAVA FALLS

Much farther downriver, at mile 179.6, Lava Falls awaits. For sheer force and speed, Lava Falls is the most impressive rapid along the entire Colorado River. It drops nearly 40 feet in a quarter mile and contains waves that can swallow boats whole, stand them on end, or flip them upside down. Just about anything can happen at Lava Falls.

The approach seems to take hours. To relieve pent-up anxiety, and as a plea to the river gods, passengers lean from their boats to kiss Vulcan's Anvil. This black hulk of volcanic rock juts out of the river in the huge pool that extends a mile upstream from Lava.

Guides spend plenty of time scouting Lava Falls because the entry—the proverbial "bubble line"—is critical. When the discussions have ended and the order of boats is determined, the inevitable moment arrives. Boats slam into thundering waves and disappear into monumental troughs, oars are popped, and sometimes guides are thrown from their seats. It's a tumultuous run, but it's over in a flash. At the bottom of Lava, with all boats right side up, every river party holds a great celebration in camp that night.

As exhilarating as the big water can be, the Colorado River has another side to its personality. Long stretches of quiet water serve as calm counterpoints to the rambunctious rapids. While floating along in these slow stretches, there is time for contemplation and observation. A buckskin deer steps silently up to the water's edge for a drink. Bighorn sheep are spotted high on a slope, in perfect camouflage against the buff-colored land. A great blue heron takes wing. A beaver leaves a trace on the sandy banks. The reflections on the silky water are molten copper and indigo blue.

This is when the Colorado River and its Grand Canyon can change a person: when an invisible line is crossed and a mere vacation becomes the journey of a lifetime; when the river and the canyon become that land of music and song.

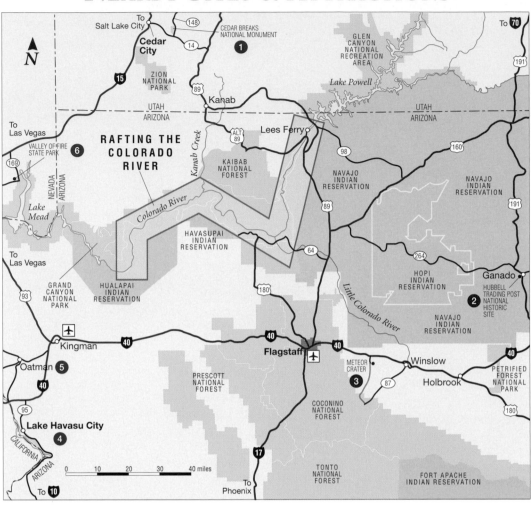

Viewed from above, Meteor Crater appears to be a small depression in the Mojave Desert. The top of the crater is in fact 60 stories tall.

① CEDAR BREAKS NATIONAL MONUMENT, UTAH

Established in 1933 as a national monument, Cedar Breaks is a huge rock amphitheater, gouged out of the earth by millions of years of uplift and erosion by water, wind, and ice. This natural coliseum is more than 2,000 feet deep and approximately three miles in diameter. Among its many unusual natural limestone formations are spires, columns, arches, and canyons. Traces of iron and manganese give the rock its varying hues of red, yellow, and purple; the colors change according to how light plays on them. A five-mile road along the rim affords panoramic views of the cliffs and the high country. Stunted bristlecone pines have adapted to the harsh growing conditions of the basin and cling to the ridges. Although no trails lead into the basin, there are two hiking trails along the rim. In summer, wildflowers carpet the nearby meadowlands. Located 23 miles from Cedar City via Hwys. 14 and 148.

② HUBBELL TRADING POST NATIONAL HISTORIC SITE, ARIZONA

This 160-acre homestead and trading post was established in 1876 by trader John Hubbell. It soon became a center for ranchers and Navajo Indians in the region. Hubbell earned the trust of the Navajos through his familiarity with their customs and language. When his land was incorporated into the Navajo Reservation, he was allowed to keep his homestead. The trading post was operated by his family until 1967, when it was purchased by the National Park Service. The post is still open for business, selling many of the traditional crafts of the Navajo, Zuni, and Hopi Indians, including turquoise-and-silver jewelry, multicolored Navajo blankets, pottery, and hand-woven baskets, as well as groceries and hardware items. Visitors can tour Hubbell's house and barn. Located 1 mile south of Ganado on Hwy. 264.

③ METEOR CRATER, ARIZONA

One of the best-preserved meteorite sites on the planet, this gigantic crater resulted from the force of impact of a meteorite that fell to earth approximately 50,000 years ago. Traveling at a speed of about 40,000 miles an hour, the meteorite created a vast chasm 550 feet deep, 4,000 feet wide, and with a circumference of more than 2.4 miles. The Museum of Astrogeology provides visitors with a self-guided tour and video presentations that explain the origins of meteorites. A huge, 1,406-pound meteorite—the largest one found in the region—is on display in the museum. The topography of Meteor Crater closely resembles that of the moon, and in 1963 the crater became a training site for Apollo astronauts preparing for the moon landing. The Astronaut Hall of Fame displays an Apollo space capsule, as well as exhibits on the exploration of space. Located 35 miles east of Flagstaff off Hwy. 40.

4 LAKE HAVASU CITY, ARIZONA

Incorporated in 1964, Lake Havasu City gained public attention in 1971 when its founder, the late Robert McCulloch, purchased historic London Bridge from the city of London for almost $2.5 million and had it moved to Lake Havasu. A total of 10,276 granite blocks were carefully labeled, transported by ship, and reassembled in their new location. The reconstructed bridge connects an island in Lake Havasu with the mainland. An English-style village has been built beside the bridge, complete with pub, restaurant, and shops; a red double-decker bus is parked on the waterfront. Located 19 miles south of Hwy. 40 on Hwy. 95.

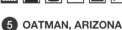

5 OATMAN, ARIZONA

The town, which is located on old Route 66, takes its name from a pioneer family that was attacked by Indians near Gila Bend. Founded in 1906, Oatman was a gold-mining town that also served as a business center for several communities in the region. During its boom years, Oatman boasted 20 saloons and 12,000 inhabitants. By 1942 almost 1.8 million ounces of gold had been extracted from the area,

and another western ghost town was born. Many of Oatman's original buildings still stand, and wild burros—descendants of those used by the first prospectors—roam freely through the town. The Oatman Museum is housed in the old Oatman Hotel, the only two-story adobe building in the county. The museum displays photographs and artifacts that depict the town's colorful history. The former town jail also houses exhibits on the history of the area. Located between Kingman and Needles on Hwy. 66.

6 VALLEY OF FIRE STATE PARK, NEVADA

Nevada's oldest state park is named for the unusual red and gold sandstone formations—the remnants of ancient seashores—that were shaped about 150 million years ago by the eroding forces of wind and water. The eight-mile-long valley can be explored on foot or by car. A self-guiding trail through Petroglyph Canyon allows visitors to view ancient Indian rock carvings. Scenic Loop Road takes in some of the park's most intriguing features, such as Arch Rock, Piano Rock, the Beehives, and the Seven Sisters. A short walking trail leads to Elephant Rock, one of the park's best-known natural sculptures. Two interpretive trails lead to the petrified remains of the forests that covered the area 225 million years ago. In springtime, the park roads are lined with desert marigold, indigo bush, desert mallow, and other blossoming plants. A visitor center provides displays on the geology, ecology, and history of the region. The Lost City Museum, in nearby Overton, exhibits some of the pottery and other artifacts of the different Indian cultures that lived in the region. The park is located 55 miles northeast of Las Vegas on Hwys. 15 and 169.

A gnarled bristlecone pine thrives in Cedar Breaks National Monument, despite the arid terrain. One bristlecone pine in the area has survived for more than 1,600 years.

Sunlight accents the golden- and reddish-hued cliffs in Valley of Fire State Park.

DURANGO & SILVERTON NARROW GAUGE RAILROAD

*A ride on this enterprising living monument
to America's past is an exciting trip
back to the past century.*

Long ago cut off from the nation's rail network, this scant 45 miles of track through the rugged peaks of the San Juans is a remnant of a mountain frontier, the mines it once served played out. But these days, the Durango & Silverton Narrow Gauge Railroad (D&SNG) breathes new life into the route—taking travelers from the sagebrush-dotted foothills of the San Juans all the way up to the high country of tall conifers and majestic alpine vistas.

The train chugs back and forth in south-western Colorado between the town of Durango and the tiny town of Silverton. Like a narrow footpath, the tracks slip through the San Juans, a remote section of the Rockies dominated by lofty peaks. Though the train still hauls a little freight, these days it mainly transports tourists through canyons and past waterfalls.

Typically, passengers sign on for an all-day, round-trip journey departing from Durango. Durango is a good jumping-off point because the town was a creation of the Denver & Rio Grande Railway, the ancestral company that laid the track now used by the D&SNG. Eager to shuttle silver ore down from the San Juans, the Denver & Rio Grande decided to build a town to serve as the southern terminus for their planned line to Silverton. In September 1880 survey stakes sprouted in the Animas River Valley, and Durango was born. Fed a rich diet of silver, the town boomed to a population of 2,500, and by March 1881, Durango boasted one church and 59 places where a thirsty miner or railroad worker could buy liquor. Construction of the spur to Silverton began in October 1881, and the line was finished in early July 1882.

DURANGO'S DEPOT

Built in 1881, the historic depot is as old as the railroad itself. This transportation hub originally was designated for Animas City, but plans fell apart after a dispute between the town council and railroad officials. As a result, in 1880 the railroad company built a new town two miles south of Animas City and named it Durango, after a city in central Mexico.

SCENERY FOR SIGHTSEERS

Overleaf: A puffing black locomotive hauls the cars of the Durango & Silverton Narrow Gauge Railroad through the emerald wilderness of the San Juan National Forest. Youngest range of the Rockies, the rugged San Juan Mountains are also the steepest.

Many of the buildings and some of the flavor of Durango's early years still can be found in the old part of town, around the D&SNG depot. Beautiful Victorian homes and commercial buildings line the Main Avenue and Third Avenue historic districts. Contemporary Durango also has its merits. Besides having more churches and fewer saloons (per capita, anyway) than it did in 1881, this town of 13,000 offers many recreational opportunities, such as river rafting, horseback riding, golfing, jeeping, and mountain biking.

| BEHIND THE SCENES AT THE DEPOT | Passengers must board the train at least 30 minutes prior to departure, but it's well worth arriving even earlier in order to savor the atmosphere. |

An hour-long tour of the railroad yard offers a behind-the-scenes look at the massive turntable, the locomotive repair shop, and the roundhouse. The original depot is little changed since 1881. Many of the coach cars are of similar vintage, and those that are newer were faithfully built in the 1880's style. The cars feature fine craftsmanship and lovely details, such as maple paneling and mahogany moldings. In addition, the D&SNG includes open-air observation cars of more recent construction; a fancy, historic parlor car open to adults only (alcohol is served); an equally old caboose that has been re-fitted to carry passengers; and sumptuous private cars that can be rented and hitched to the end of the train.

INFORMATION FOR VISITORS

From Denver, take Hwy. 70 to Grand Junction and then go south on Hwy. 50 and Hwy. 550 to Durango. Or take Hwy. 25 south from Denver to Walsenburg and then travel west on Hwy. 160 to Durango. The Durango & Silverton Narrow Gauge Railroad operates year-round except for about three weeks in November and on Christmas Day. Due to occasional snow slides between Durango and Silverton, the one daily winter train goes instead to Cascade Canyon and back—a round trip of 52 miles. During the summer season (roughly May through October), several trains make the 90-mile round trip from Durango to Silverton daily. By arrangement, passengers can stay in Silverton overnight and return on a different train. A private bus company also provides service from Silverton back to Durango, allowing travelers to travel only one way by train. By special arrangement, the train will drop off and pick up backpackers. Adult passengers can book space in the parlor car; lavish private cars and a caboose are also available for rent. Reservations should be made four to six weeks in advance.

For more information: D&SNG, 479 Main Ave., Durango, CO 81301. (970) 247-2733.

FURTIVE FAUN

With eyes and ears alert for signs of danger, a mule deer surveys the view from grass level. Although hunting nearly wiped them out during the past century, mule deer once again thrive in the San Juan Mountains.

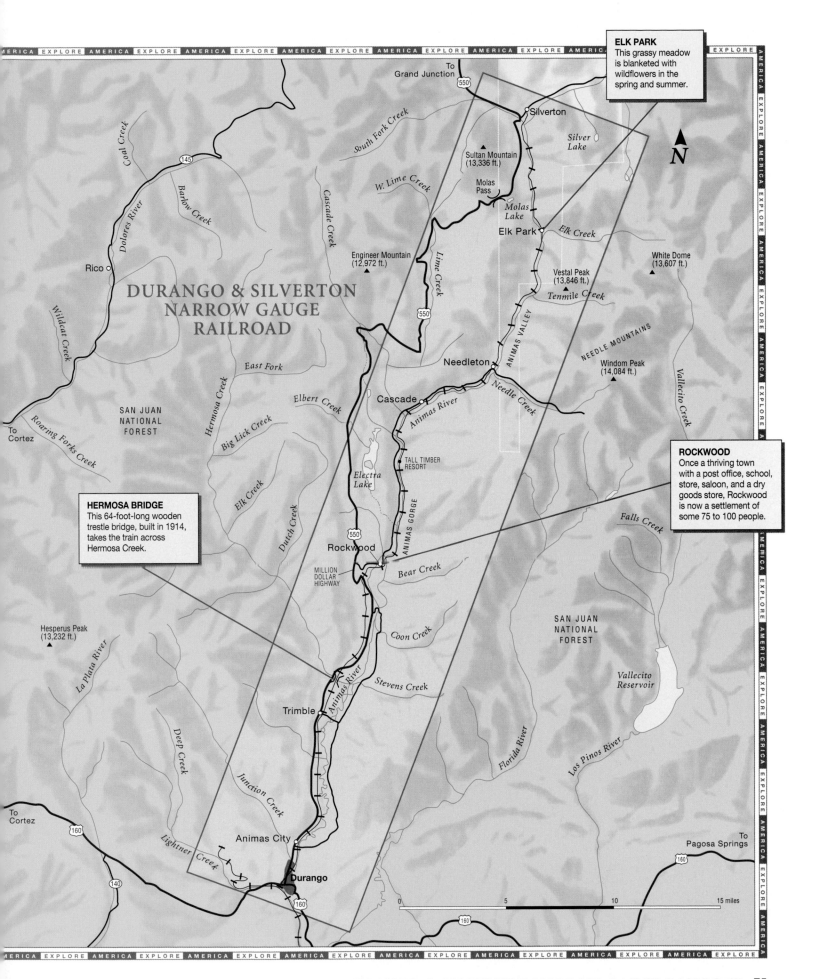

DURANGO & SILVERTON NARROW GAUGE RAILROAD

ELK PARK
This grassy meadow is blanketed with wildflowers in the spring and summer.

ROCKWOOD
Once a thriving town with a post office, school, store, saloon, and a dry goods store, Rockwood is now a settlement of some 75 to 100 people.

HERMOSA BRIDGE
This 64-foot-long wooden trestle bridge, built in 1914, takes the train across Hermosa Creek.

To Grand Junction

Silverton

Silver Lake

Sultan Mountain (13,336 ft.)

Molas Pass

Molas Lake

Elk Park

Elk Creek

White Dome (13,607 ft.)

Engineer Mountain (12,972 ft.)

Vestal Peak (13,846 ft.)

Tenmile Creek

Coal Creek

Barlow Creek

Dolores River

South Fork Creek

W. Lime Creek

Cascade Creek

Lime Creek

Rico

Wildcat Creek

East Fork

Elbert Creek

Needleton

Animas Valley

Needle Mountains

Windom Peak (14,084 ft.)

Vallecito Creek

Needle Creek

Cascade

Animas River

SAN JUAN NATIONAL FOREST

To Cortez

Roaring Forks Creek

Hermosa Creek

Big Lick Creek

Elk Creek

Dutch Creek

Electra Lake

TALL TIMBER RESORT

ANIMAS GORGE

Falls Creek

Rockwood

MILLION DOLLAR HIGHWAY

Bear Creek

SAN JUAN NATIONAL FOREST

Vallecito Reservoir

Hesperus Peak (13,232 ft.)

La Plata River

Deep Creek

Coon Creek

Stevens Creek

Florida River

Los Pinos River

Trimble

Animas River

Junction Creek

To Cortez

Lightner Creek

Animas City

Durango

To Pagosa Springs

0   5   10   15 miles

N

The king of the D&SNG's equipment rumbles
into view about 15 minutes before departure,
proudly puffing past the passenger cars and assum-
ing its rightful place at the head of the train. The
engine "puffs" because all six D&SNG engines are
genuine coal-fired, steam-powered locomotives
built more than 70 years ago; it's easy to imagine
Casey Jones at the throttle.

**THREE-HOUR
JOURNEY**

Right on schedule, the conductor cries "All aboard!" and
the three-hour journey to
Silverton begins. The whistle
blows and the mighty locomotive strains forward.
The burly driver wheels start turning and the engine
emits those chuffing exhalations that are as familiar a sound out West as the mournful howl of a
coyote or the crack of a Colt .45. As the train heads
out of town and up the bucolic Animas Valley,
passengers gaze at wildflowers, grazing horses, a
waterfall, and the so-called red-beds—the husky
hills whose mineral-laden soil gleams a rich rust
color in the sunlight. This is a good time to just

lean back and soak up the ambience of the train: the excited talk of fellow passengers, the rush of fresh air, the gentle swaying motion, and the familiar clickity-clack of riding the rails.

About a dozen miles out of Durango, the train begins climbing the west side of the valley. Tan-and-gray limestone cliffs form a backdrop for scrub oaks, piñon pines, and a scattering of yellow-barked ponderosa pines. A few miles later, just beyond the ghost town of Rockwood, the train eases through a cut made in a hillside of red granite. A movie crew covered this cut to simulate a tunnel for the 1956 film *Around the World in 80 Days*.

Just a few hundred yards beyond, the engineer slows the train down to a crawl while traversing the High Line—the name bestowed upon the half-mile stretch of track that tiptoes along the edge of the most rugged part of Animas Canyon. Railroad crews painstakingly carved out a ledge on which to lay the tracks by using black powder to blast through the stubborn granite. Some of the holes drilled in the rock to hold the powder charges are still visible.

In places the ledge is only eight feet wide. The need to squeeze the train through such tight passages accounts for the Denver & Rio Grande's choice of narrow gauge tracks, which are only three feet apart rather than the standard four feet, eight-and-a-half inches. This tightrope of track, 400 feet above the rushing rapids of the Animas River, provides some dizzying views, especially for passengers brave enough to peer down into the sheer gorges below.

A few miles past the Animas Gorge, the train makes a brief stop at Tall Timber Resort, which can be reached only by rail. At this point the resort's name makes sense: the train has climbed above 7,500 feet and high-country vegetation is taking over. The valley that cups Tall Timber is ringed by mountains bristling with Douglas fir, spruce, sub-alpine fir, and limber pine. Also common are "quakies" (quaking aspen), their delicate oval leaves dancing at the slightest breeze. Quakies fill the valley and form light green patches amid the deep green of the mountainside conifer forests. As autumn approaches those trillions of oval leaves

turn a radiant gold. Scanning the ground beneath the aspens, sharp-eyed passengers can spot blue columbines, Colorado's state flower.

<table>
<tr><td>MAJESTIC
MOUNTAINS</td><td>For many miles passengers have been teased by distant glimpses of the Olympian peaks of the San Juans. Just</td></tr>
</table>

For many miles passengers have been teased by distant glimpses of the Olympian peaks of the San Juans. Just past Tall Timber the pinnacles parade into full view. Looming to the northeast are Windom Peak, Vestal Peak, White Dome, and the other 13,000- to 14,000-foot colossi of the Needle Mountains. During the last ice age, glaciers moved through the San Juans, gouging out valleys and sanding mountains smooth. But the tips of the highest peaks stayed above the ice fields, escaping the glacial grind and thereby remaining sharp, cathedral-like spires.

Mining flourished briefly in the shadows of these peaks. The train passes the site of Needleton, an old mining camp that roared into life in 1882 and faded by the turn of the century. The Black Giant, the Mastodon, the Little Jim, as well as many other abandoned mines burrow deep into the mountain slopes in this area.

Half a mile farther on, the train goes by the Needleton Snow Slide, the most southerly of the many avalanche chutes along the route. Virtually every winter, tsunamis of snow careen down these steep runs and bury the track. Summer passengers can see the avalanche scars: ragged vertical grooves where trees and shrubs have been scraped away. Back when the railroad was Silverton's lifeline, crews fought to keep the line open in winter. Often it was a losing battle: in 1891, slides blocked the tracks for 51 days straight. Sometimes when the snow got too deep to remove, the crews would cut a train-size tunnel through it.

From late November until the beginning of the main season—around May 1—the D&SNG runs a daily train into the winter wonderland of the San Juans. Although a passenger train did get stranded by snow slides for 10 days in 1906, today's passengers needn't worry. The winter train goes only 26 miles up to Cascade Canyon, where it turns around before reaching the avalanche areas and heads back to Durango.

The 15-mile stretch of track between the old Needleton mining camp and the town of Silverton features glorious high-country landscape: jagged peaks by the score, glacier-burnished cliffs, tributary creeks cascading into the Animas River, willow-framed beaver ponds, and broad meadows beaming with primroses, asters, goldenrod, and Indian paintbrush. The train ascends at an appropriately leisurely pace through this striking scenery, giving passengers plenty of time to savor the vistas. Finally the tracks level out at 9,300 feet in Silverton, the end of the line.

AUTUMN TAPESTRY

Set off by a crisp blue sky, a mountainside of aspen trees in the San Juans blaze gold and red in the fall. These graceful trees grow to about 80 feet tall.

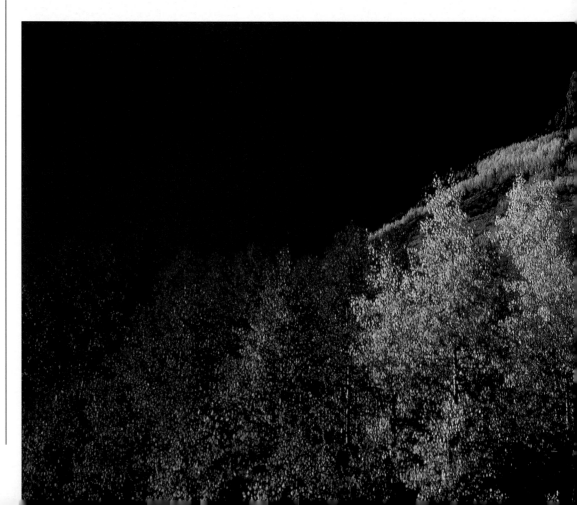

SILVERTON'S SPLENDOR

The train stops for two hours in this town of 500, which is set in a pretty little valley cradled by broad-shouldered mountains. One could easily spend the time just imbibing the beauty of the surroundings, but it would be a shame not to explore one of the nation's best-preserved Old West mining towns. Unlike most towns of its period, Silverton never was ravaged by a major fire, so present-day visitors can find much to relish: the entire town is a National Historic Landmark. Many of Silverton's finer buildings were erected in the early 1900's. Among the highlights are the stately County Courthouse, the Carnegie Library, the newly restored Town Hall,

and the old jail, which now houses the San Juan County Historical Museum. Many of the venerable buildings are still active concerns, such as the Grand Imperial Hotel, where visitors can lunch while ogling the century-old cherrywood bar and the pressed-tin ceiling. The restored Rio Grande Depot, built in 1882, is still used as the ticket office for the D&SNG.

Although Silverton may be the end of the line, it's not the end of the trip. All too soon, the train whistle sounds four long and loud blasts, summoning passengers back to the train for the return trip to Durango. Once more the conductor shouts "All aboard!" the whistle blows, and the locomotive surges ahead, emitting the chuffing exhalations that for more than a century have signaled the start of a great adventure.

MILLION-DOLLAR VIEW
A flock of sheep meanders through Molas Pass, located at an elevation of about 10,000 feet. The pass is on the Million Dollar Highway—a breathtaking road that twists and turns as it climbs high into the San Juans, offering visitors another way to marvel at the scenery.

NEARBY SITES & ATTRACTIONS

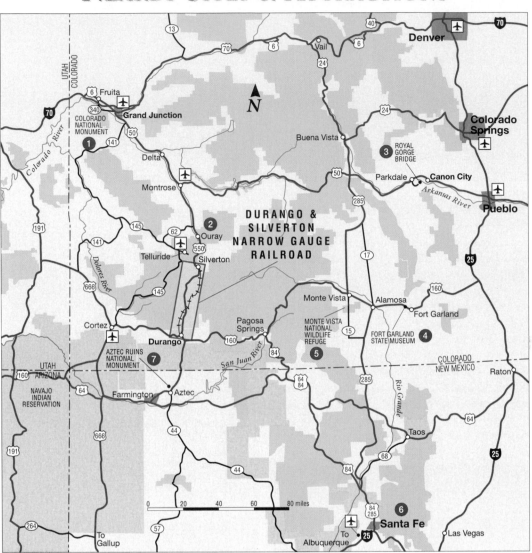

Wright's Opera House in Ouray was built in 1888 by Edward Wright, who made his money at the Wheel of Fortune Mine. The opera house was patronized by the town's more refined families. Built in the Romanesque Revival style, the building has an interesting decorative iron facade.

1 COLORADO NATIONAL MONUMENT

This 20,450-acre park protects a landscape of 500-foot-deep canyons, natural arches, and towering monoliths. One of these, Independence Monument, is a 350-foot-high rock that rises from the canyon floor like an ancient spire. Etched into the Uncompahgre Highland by the combined forces of wind and rain, the multihued sandstone walls of the canyons display billions of years of geological history. Because its magnificent formations are similar to the Grand Canyon and are relatively accessible, the park is a favorite among both amateur and professional geologists. A visitor center offers exhibits and a slide program. Rim Rock Drive, a 23-mile paved road, offers panoramic views of the canyon scenery. A network of hiking trails zigzags across mesas and down into the canyons. Serpents Trail, named for the 54 switchbacks along its length, is one of the most popular trails. The park harbors a variety of wildlife, including mountain lions, mule deer, and bighorn sheep. Located 2½ miles south of Fruita on Hwy. 340.

2 OURAY, COLORADO

Nicknamed the Switzerland of America because of its majestic setting in the San Juan Mountains, Ouray is an old mining town founded in 1876 when two prospectors traveling north from Silverton discovered gold. Most of Ouray's buildings were built during the town's boom period, which lasted from 1880 to 1900. A walking tour allows visitors to view the finely preserved turn-of-the-century architecture. Elks Lodge is one of the highlights of the tour and one of the most peculiar buildings in Ouray: the building combines features of French, Queen Anne, and Romanesque architecture. The town was named after Ouray, chief of the Ute Indians, who enjoyed the waters of Ouray's natural hot springs. Today the hot springs are pumped into the 250-by-150-foot Ouray Hot Springs Pool, a public pool whose waters range from 80° to 103°F. Four-wheel drive, bicycle, and hiking trails are popular ways of exploring the nearby scenery. In the winter, the region offers alpine and cross-country skiing. Located on Hwy. 550.

3 ROYAL GORGE BRIDGE, COLORADO

In 1907 Congress allocated control of the Royal Gorge to the municipality of Canon City, stipulating that the gorge be used for recreational purposes only. The city felt that the best way to allow visitors to see this natural wonder would be to build a bridge across it. Construction of a suspension bridge—the world's highest—began in 1929 and was completed just six months later. A marvel of engineering, the 1,053-foot-high Royal Gorge Bridge provides a dramatic view of the gorge and the raging Arkansas River, which courses through it, for motorists and pedestrians alike. The world's steepest funicular railway also takes visitors into the heart of the gorge, traveling 1,550 feet at a 45° angle. An aerial tramway, added to the bridge in 1969, traverses its length at an elevation of 1,178 feet, offering panoramic views of the gorge and the bridge. Located 8 miles west of Canon City off Hwy. 50.

4 FORT GARLAND STATE MUSEUM, COLORADO

Built to protect early settlers in the region from attacks by the Ute Indians, this remote military outpost operated for a quarter of a century, beginning in 1858. The single-story walled adobe fort was capable of housing up to two companies of infantrymen and riflemen, who honed their skills in the central parade ground. Kit Carson, a colonel with the 1st New Mexico Cavalry and one of the West's most famed frontiersmen, was in charge of a volunteer regiment at Fort Garland from 1866 to 1867. The structure has been restored and is a superb example of the architectural style of adobe frontier forts. Visitors can tour the commandant's quarters, which have been furnished much as they would have been in Carson's time. There are also displays on military life at the fort, including a collection of uniforms and weapons. Located outside the town of Fort Garland off Hwy. 160.

5 MONTE VISTA NATIONAL WILDLIFE REFUGE, COLORADO

Located in the San Luis Valley, the refuge was established in 1953 to protect a wetland habitat for migratory birds and other wildlife. Although the San Luis Valley receives very little precipitation, spring thaw brings melted snow waters from the San Juan Mountains. These waters feed into the Rio Grande and raise the valley's water table, creating an ideal environment for a great number of water birds. During the summer, bird-watchers can spot common nighthawks, red-shafted flickers, and sage thrashers; in the winter, the refuge provides a temporary home to northern harriers, bald and golden eagles, ring-necked pheasants, and dark-eyed juncos. Springtime brings the most feathered visitors to the refuge, including great blue herons, mourning doves, yellow-rumped warblers, and up to 5,000 sandhill cranes. As well as local country roads, there is a three-mile drive through a section of the refuge and numerous walking trails. Located 6 miles south of Monte Vista on Hwy. 15.

6 SANTA FE, NEW MEXICO

The capital of New Mexico, Santa Fe was originally settled by Pueblo Indians around A.D. 1050. In 1609 the town was established by Spanish settlers. In the early 19th century, when Mexico gained independence from Spain, trade opened between the United States and Santa Fe by way of the Santa Fe Trail. Today the blend of cultures is still evident, especially in the city's architecture—a mixture of Spanish pueblo and traditional territorial styles. One of the city's most famous buildings is the Cathedral of St. Francis of Assisi, built between 1869 and 1886 on the ruins of a Spanish church that was destroyed in the 1680 Pueblo Revolt. Santa Fe has long been known for its arts community; painter Georgia O'Keefe is one of many artists to call Santa Fe home. The city has museums dedicated to the fine arts and to folk art, a wide range of art galleries, several dance companies, and a world-class opera company. Located on Hwys. 285 and 84.

7 AZTEC RUINS NATIONAL MONUMENT, NEW MEXICO

Convinced that the ruins were of Aztec origin, early Anglo settlers misnamed this site. Archeologists now know that the Anasazi lived here. The monument preserves several room blocks, earth mounds, refuse heaps, roadways, and associated artifacts. The West Ruin, a massive structure of approximately 450 interconnected rooms built in the early 1100's, has been mostly excavated. Its thick stone and mud walls rise three stories in some places. Original roofs of wood logs and splints cover several rooms. The Great Kiva, in the central plaza, is a large, partially underground ceremonial structure. This reconstructed building is fully roofed and contains many of the features found during the original excavations of 1921. Aztec Ruins was named a national monument in 1923 and proclaimed a World Heritage Site in 1987. A self-guiding trail winds through the West Ruin. A visitor center offers exhibits and video presentations about the site. Located 1½ miles north of Aztec off Hwy. 550.

Dubbed the Grand Canyon of the Arkansas, the jagged granite walls of the Royal Gorge rise 1,053 feet above the Arkansas River. Seen from a distance, the Royal Gorge Bridge looks like a tightrope strung from rim to rim.

Early morning light bathes the three-story walls of the West Ruin at Aztec Ruins National Monument. This ancient Anasazi settlement is one of the best-preserved pueblo ruins in the Southwest.

THE COAST STARLIGHT

America's Pacific Coast unfolds beyond coach windows for travelers with an eye for variety and beauty.

At historic Union Station in Los Angeles, an announcement comes over the loudspeakers: "Your attention, please. This will be the first call for Amtrak train Number Fourteen, the *Coast Starlight*, departing for Oxnard, Santa Barbara, San Luis Obispo, Salinas, San Jose, Oakland, Sacramento, Klamath Falls, Eugene, Tacoma, Portland, and Seattle." The song of those place-names as well of stops along the way hints at the scope of the journey that lies ahead—downtown skyscrapers and skyscraping forests; beaches thronged by sunbathers and beaches populated only by sandpipers; vast cities where millions of people speed down the fast lane and small towns where residents rock on their front porches; lofty mountaintops swathed in snow and desert grasslands sprinkled with sagebrush.

Some of the enticing places served by the *Coast Starlight* can be enjoyed even before the train departs. Surrounding Union Station is El Pueblo de Nuestra Señora la Reina de los Angeles, better known as the city of Los Angeles. The full name

EXPLORE AMERICA EXPLORE AMERICA EXPLORE AMERI

OFFSHORE INHABITANTS
Channel Islands National Park provides a safe haven for a diversity of wildlife, including sea lions, seen here frolicking on a rock. The five rugged islands that comprise the park lie within reach of the coast of Southern California.

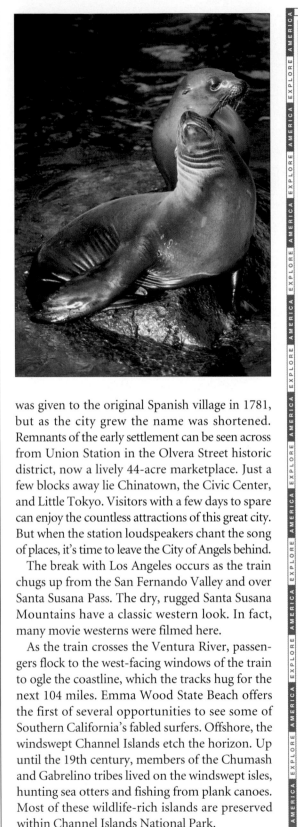

PACIFIC VIEWS
Overleaf: An impressive elevated trestle bridge links up a section of the coastal railroad as it travels through Gaviota State Park, which is located northwest of Santa Barbara. Gaviota *is Spanish for "seagull," many of which swoop and soar along the shoreline of the Pacific Ocean.*

INFORMATION FOR VISITORS

The Coast Starlight departs from Los Angeles and Seattle daily. Fares vary widely, depending on seat availability. The one-way trip of 1,389 miles takes 35 hours to complete. The train is equipped with coach cars, private sleeping compartments, a dining car, and a sightseer lounge; reservations are required for coach and sleeping cars. Among the train's scheduled stops are Santa Barbara, Oakland (San Francisco is connected by a shuttle bus), Sacramento, Klamath Falls, Eugene, Portland, Tacoma, and Seattle. Passengers can make stopovers at any of these cities. Major airports are located at Los Angeles, Oakland–San Francisco, Portland, and Seattle. For more information: Coast Starlight, Amtrak West, 800 North Alameda Street, Los Angeles, CA 90012. (800) 872-7245.

was given to the original Spanish village in 1781, but as the city grew the name was shortened. Remnants of the early settlement can be seen across from Union Station in the Olvera Street historic district, now a lively 44-acre marketplace. Just a few blocks away lie Chinatown, the Civic Center, and Little Tokyo. Visitors with a few days to spare can enjoy the countless attractions of this great city. But when the station loudspeakers chant the song of places, it's time to leave the City of Angels behind.

The break with Los Angeles occurs as the train chugs up from the San Fernando Valley and over Santa Susana Pass. The dry, rugged Santa Susana Mountains have a classic western look. In fact, many movie westerns were filmed here.

As the train crosses the Ventura River, passengers flock to the west-facing windows of the train to ogle the coastline, which the tracks hug for the next 104 miles. Emma Wood State Beach offers the first of several opportunities to see some of Southern California's fabled surfers. Offshore, the windswept Channel Islands etch the horizon. Up until the 19th century, members of the Chumash and Gabrelino tribes lived on the windswept isles, hunting sea otters and fishing from plank canoes. Most of these wildlife-rich islands are preserved within Channel Islands National Park.

In Santa Barbara, the station's grounds are home to the colossal Moreton Bay Fig Tree, planted in 1877. Reportedly, more than 10,000 people can stand in its shade at noon. Passengers can disembark and admire the sailboats bobbing at anchor in Santa Barbara's pretty harbor, stroll its palm-lined

STYLISH STATION
Los Angeles' Union Station is an architectural blend of Spanish and Art Deco styles. Built in 1939, the station is commonly referred to as the Union Station Passenger Terminal.

EXPLORE AMERICA EXPLORE AMERICA EXPLORE AMER

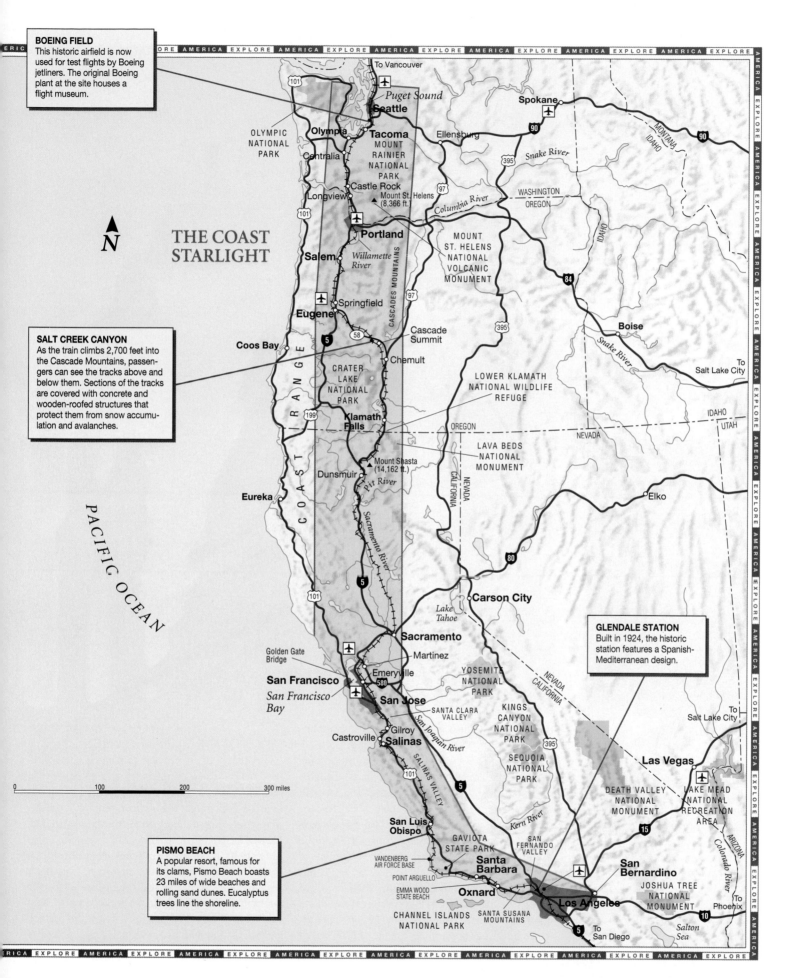

BOEING FIELD
This historic airfield is now used for test flights by Boeing jetliners. The original Boeing plant at the site houses a flight museum.

THE COAST STARLIGHT

SALT CREEK CANYON
As the train climbs 2,700 feet into the Cascade Mountains, passengers can see the tracks above and below them. Sections of the tracks are covered with concrete and wooden-roofed structures that protect them from snow accumulation and avalanches.

GLENDALE STATION
Built in 1924, the historic station features a Spanish-Mediterranean design.

PISMO BEACH
A popular resort, famous for its clams, Pismo Beach boasts 23 miles of wide beaches and rolling sand dunes. Eucalyptus trees line the shoreline.

PACIFIC OCEAN

To Vancouver
Puget Sound
Seattle
Spokane
Olympia
Tacoma
Ellensburg
OLYMPIC NATIONAL PARK
Centralia
MOUNT RAINIER NATIONAL PARK
Castle Rock
Longview
Mount St. Helens (8,366 ft.)
Columbia River
WASHINGTON
OREGON
Portland
MOUNT ST. HELENS NATIONAL VOLCANIC MONUMENT
Salem
Willamette River
CASCADES MOUNTAINS
Springfield
Eugene
Cascade Summit
Coos Bay
Chemult
CRATER LAKE NATIONAL PARK
LOWER KLAMATH NATIONAL WILDLIFE REFUGE
COAST RANGE
Klamath Falls
OREGON
IDAHO
NEVADA
UTAH
Mount Shasta (14,162 ft.)
Dunsmuir
LAVA BEDS NATIONAL MONUMENT
Pit River
Eureka
CALIFORNIA
NEVADA
Elko
Sacramento River
Carson City
Lake Tahoe
Sacramento
Martinez
Golden Gate Bridge
Emeryville
YOSEMITE NATIONAL PARK
San Francisco
San Francisco Bay
San Jose
SANTA CLARA VALLEY
KINGS CANYON NATIONAL PARK
Gilroy
Castroville
Salinas
San Joaquin River
SEQUOIA NATIONAL PARK
SALINAS VALLEY
San Luis Obispo
Kern River
DEATH VALLEY NATIONAL MONUMENT
LAKE MEAD NATIONAL RECREATION AREA
Las Vegas
GAVIOTA STATE PARK
SAN FERNANDO VALLEY
VANDENBERG AIR FORCE BASE
Santa Barbara
San Bernardino
JOSHUA TREE NATIONAL MONUMENT
POINT ARGUELLO
EMMA WOOD STATE BEACH
Oxnard
Los Angeles
CHANNEL ISLANDS NATIONAL PARK
SANTA SUSANA MOUNTAINS
To San Diego
Salton Sea
To Phoenix
To Salt Lake City
Boise
Snake River
MONTANA
IDAHO
To Salt Lake City

0   100   200   300 miles

Because of its hilltop setting and gracious sandstone buildings, Mission Santa Barbara is nicknamed Queen of the Missions. Much of the city of Santa Barbara features the whitewashed walls and red-tiled roofs that are characteristic of mission architecture.

FEATHERED FISHERMAN
Usually sighted in large groups along the California coast, the double-crested cormorant's short, strong legs make this seabird a powerful swimmer and an efficient fisher.

boulevards, and inspect the daily catch at the open-air fish market on historic Stearns Wharf.

The wharf is just one of the many landmarks for which Santa Barbara is noted. Chumash Indians occupied the site for centuries, but the Spanish colonial era most influenced the city's character. In the center of town, El Presidio de Santa Barbara State Historic Park contains reconstructed adobe buildings from the original Spanish settlement of 1782. Foremost among the venerable buildings from colonial days is Mission Santa Barbara, which overlooks the city from a low ridge of the Santa Ynez Mountains. The mission's beautiful sandstone buildings are among the best preserved of California's 21 Franciscan missions.

WEST COAST VIEWS

As the *Coast Starlight* heads northwest from Santa Barbara, it soon passes the "cricket" pumps of the Ellwood Oil Field. In 1942 a Japanese submarine fired 17 rounds from its deck gun at the oil field, making it the site of the only direct enemy attack on the continental United States in modern history. Here the landscape consists of long stretches of undeveloped shoreline and coastal marsh. Brown pelicans glide over the surface of the sea, then plunge into the water in pursuit of fish. Just beyond the surf, vast kelp forests sway in the currents below the surface. Inland, the grassy hills are wrinkled by gullies and sprinkled with oak trees.

The train leaves the coast highway and all other roads behind as the tracks snake along ocean bluffs. For the next hour or so, passengers can savor a view of 50 miles of wild shoreline; large ranches and sprawling Vandenberg Air Force Base have precluded development of this coast. Harbor seals sun on offshore rocks. During spring and fall, migrating gray whales heave through the water beyond the surf. And right below the tracks, waves crash on sandy beaches or explode against rocks. Many a ship has also crashed against the rocks here, particularly near Point Arguello. In 1923 the fog was so thick that a flotilla of seven U.S. Navy destroyers ran aground. Just north of the point is the massive launch pad and tower built to serve the space shuttle. Other launch pads loom into sight 10 minutes later as the train passes through the base's missile test range. (Signs that say "Unexploded Shells" aren't referring to sea shells.)

The tracks then veer inland, forsaking the Pacific for the rest of the journey. For a while, the ocean's influence continues to be felt as the train winds through sand dunes and coastal marshes. Finally, near the resort town of Pismo Beach, the *Coast Starlight* makes a more definitive inland turn and forges into California's interior.

Twenty minutes off the coast, the train chugs into San Luis Obispo. In a recent national rating, this municipality was named the most livable small city in America, and it's easy to see why. One of the town's highlights is the adobe church of Mission San Luis Obispo de Tolosa, founded in 1772. The aptness of the city's number-one rating is sealed as the *Coast Starlight* slowly begins its climb out of town along the sweeping Horseshoe Curves—the rugged, poppy-bedecked hills that provide the town with its lovely setting.

For the next few hours, the train winds through prime farmland: the Salinas Valley is known as the Country's Salad Bowl. Castroville bills itself as the Artichoke Capital of the World. Neighboring Gilroy claims a similar title for its garlic, and the town's annual festival boasts even garlic ice cream.

Come evening, the Santa Clara Valley gives way to Silicon Valley as the train enters San Jose, at the southern end of San Francisco Bay. As the tracks skirt the southeastern shore of the bay, passengers see a few natural areas, such as salt marshes thronged with shorebirds and waterfowl. The train makes a stop in Oakland, and passengers can look across the bay at the city's downtown spires, Alcatraz Island, and the Golden Gate Bridge.

GREEN VALLEY
Rows of lettuce attest to the fertility of the Salinas Valley, one of California's prime agricultural regions.

patchwork of lakes, marshes, rivers, and creeks. The train finally veers to the northwest just past Chemult station and heads into the high country.

As the *Coast Starlight* traverses the Cascades, it seems as if it is forging its own route. For half an hour the train slowly curves up through the trees, skirting beautiful Odell Lake, until the tracks top out above 4,800 feet at Cascade Summit. The downhill run from Cascade Summit to the town of Oakridge is even steeper, and for the next hour and a half the train seldom exceeds 30 miles an hour. The tracks burrow through 22 tunnels and numerous snow sheds during the 3,600-foot plunge to the valley, but for most of this stretch the train is out in the open and the views are spectacular.

BAY VIEW
Bedecked in bright red-orange paint, the Golden Gate Bridge spans the mile-wide entrance to San Francisco Bay. Since its opening in 1937, the bridge has become the symbol of the city of San Francisco.

Northbound *Coast Starlight* passengers see this view at night; the train doesn't reach the northern end of the Bay Area until about nine o'clock. The southbound train comes through at about seven in the morning, however, so during the longer days of summer, spring, and fall, those passengers can see the Golden Gate gleaming in the sunlight. Neither northbound nor southbound passengers get a daylight look at the nearly 300 miles between Martinez, which marks the northern limit of the Bay Area, and Dunsmuir. Most of those miles lie within the Central Valley, one of the world's most intensively worked agricultural regions.

A LANDMARK MOUNTAIN

Waking up on a train immediately elicits the question, "Where are we?" Early risers on the northbound train might see several clues: rushing rivers, some burly mountains, and conifer forests. Likely the train is around the little town of Dunsmuir, along the Sacramento River near its headwaters. Just north of Dunsmuir is one unmistakable landmark: Mount Shasta. The train passes within a few miles of this hulking volcano, giving passengers a close-up look: at 20 miles in diameter, it's the largest in the lower 48 states. For many miles the tracks cut through vast beds of volcanic rock, reminders of past cataclysms.

About the time Mount Shasta disappears from sight, the train crosses into Oregon. For most of the next 100 miles, the tracks run through a verdant

As the train edges over the Cascade Range, passengers can gaze at rocky pinnacles, old-growth forest, waterfalls, and deep canyons and valleys.

For the next 125 miles, the *Coast Starlight* rolls almost due north up the Willamette Valley. Although this is Oregon's most heavily populated region, its pastoral appearance remains largely intact. Development is concentrated in Eugene, Springfield, Salem, and Portland, leaving most of the valley a green mosaic of farms, creeks, conifer-studded hills, fruit orchards, and occasional small towns, framed by the Coast Ranges on the west and the Cascades on the east.

Oregon's only major city, Portland, lies at the northern end of the valley, where the Willamette River flows into the Columbia. The *Coast Starlight* follows the Willamette through the outskirts of Portland and crosses the river via Steel Bridge, providing grand views of the city skyline, the restored waterfront, and the ships that ply the river.

Despite a rapidly growing population, the City of Roses has retained much of its small-town charm. Pleasant neighborhoods, a modern light rail system, numerous bike paths, and a blend of historic and modern architecture contribute to Portland's appeal. Above all, it is the city's 150 leafy parks that shape Portland's character. As it pulls out of the station, the *Coast Starlight* passes 5,000-acre Forest Park, a virtual wilderness whose eastern boundary lies within a mile of downtown.

SHASTA'S MAJESTY
Mount Shasta, a 14,162-foot volcano, rises some 10,000 feet above the surrounding country-side of Northern California.

bled down the river reached this point, nearly 40 miles from Mount St. Helens. About 30 miles north of Castle Rock, on the outskirts of Centralia, passengers looking southeast can catch a glimpse of the mountain—at least what's left of it, after the eruption blew 1,300 feet off its top.

Another half an hour's journey through forest and farmland brings the *Coast Starlight* to the southern tip of Puget Sound. The tracks head up along the eastern shore, with conifer-clad hills on one side and the fecund tidal flats and open water of the sound on the other. Islands large and small appear, most of them heavily forested and lightly populated. A ferry barely big enough to tote 10 cars may pass by as it trundles from island to island. In

RIVERSIDE METROPOLIS
Portland sparkles as the lights of Tom McCall Waterfront Park and downtown office towers cast their reflection in the Willamette River. The three-mile-long riverside park is popular with joggers and cyclists and hosts many summer festivals.

PORTLAND TO SEATTLE

North of Portland, the *Coast Starlight* arcs across a long bridge that spans the Columbia River. Tiny sailboats and gargantuan tankers plow wakes in the broad river. On the north bank, huge chutes shower grain from silos into the holds of ships that will take wheat grown as far upriver as Idaho to ports on the far side of the earth.

About halfway across the main channel of the Columbia, the *Coast Starlight* enters Washington. Here the westward-flowing Columbia takes a 90-degree turn to the north, enabling the train to continue toward Seattle while still clinging precariously to the Washington side of the river. Along this 40-mile stretch of line, passengers can see the sloughs and marshes teeming with wildlife, huge rafts of logs being floated to sawmills along the river, and colorful houseboat communities.

At Longview, the Columbia River and the *Coast Starlight* part company as the river again turns west toward its inevitable rendezvous with the sea. A few minutes later the tracks lead through Castle Rock, a town undistinguished but for its status as the main gateway to Mount St. Helens National Volcanic Monument. Prior to its cataclysmic 1980 eruption, Mount St. Helens had a perfectly shaped volcanic cone, which gave it the nickname of Ice Cream Cone in the Sky. After the eruption, the cone collapsed into a gigantic crater 1,700 feet across. Just north of town the train crosses the Toutle River. When the volcano blew its top on May 18, 1980, the wave of mud and ash that rum-

the little communities, it seems that all the houses are built on pilings and everyone has a small dock and a boat house.

Things take an urban turn as the tracks approach the thriving port city of Tacoma, located at the southern tip of Puget Sound. Known until 1869 as Commencement City, Tacoma grew up around Fort Nisqually, a fur trading post set up by the Hudson's Bay Company in 1833 and now reconstructed in the city's Point Defiance Park. Tacoma was dubbed the City of Destiny by settlers lured here by the area's lumber industry. The train runs alongside Commencement Bay, flanked by the soaring peaks of the Olympic Mountains on one side and the Tacoma Narrows on the other.

Thirty miles north of Tacoma, this journey up the West Coast culminates when the *Coast Starlight* eases to a stop in Seattle—the end of the line. But the journey needn't end there. Just minutes from the train station sprawls Seattle's waterfront, where ships from around the world unload. Visitors can take in Seattle's ample attractions, ranging from the Space Needle and Pike Place Market to hidden treasures such as the Nordic Heritage Museum.

Amtrak's liberal stopover policy makes it easy to turn the Coast Starlight's 35-hour whirlwind tour into something a bit more leisurely. Whether it is hiking in the Cascades, exploring Santa Barbara's history, or strolling along Portland's waterfront, this journey has something for everyone.

SEATTLE LEGEND
Pike Place Market offers a tempting array of fresh produce grown on farms within 50 miles of Seattle. The market is also renowned for its fresh fish and seafood, some of it flown in daily from Alaska.

LONELY HEADLAND
North Head, located along the rugged coast of Washington State, is a deserted landscape of rocky outcroppings pummeled by the incessant power of the sea.

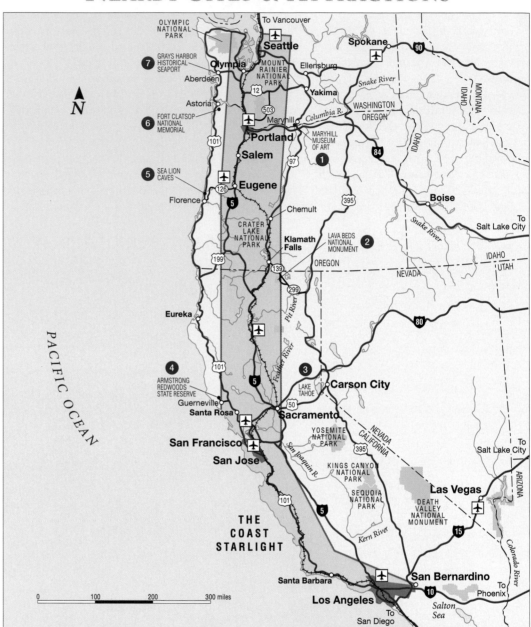

A shady walking trail in Armstrong Redwoods State Reserve allows visitors to see some of the oldest and tallest trees remaining in the state of California.

① MARYHILL MUSEUM OF ART, WASHINGTON

Set on a bluff overlooking the Columbia River, the Maryhill Museum's eclectic art exhibits include an internationally recognized collection of 52 sculptures by Auguste Rodin; furniture, jewelry, clothing, and memorabilia that once belonged to Queen Marie of Romania; more than 100 chess sets from around the world; Native American artifacts and Russian icons. Peacocks are allowed to roam freely in the 26-acre park that surrounds the museum. Maryhill was built by eccentric businessman Sam Hill. He soon lost interest in the house and turned his attention instead to building a replica of Stonehenge, located 1 mile from Maryhill. The museum opened after his death in 1940. Located 100 miles east of Portland on Hwy. 97.

② LAVA BEDS NATIONAL MONUMENT, CALIFORNIA

Forged by countless fiery volcanic eruptions, this rugged landscape consists of cinder cones, shield volcanoes, and unusual lava tube caves (formed when the outer surface of a lava flow cools faster than the interior, creating a tube). The short, one-way Cave Loop Road connects many of the caves that are open to the public. The most accessible of these is Mushpot Cave, located near the visitor center. During the summer months, park rangers conduct tours of the area. Visitors can see ancient pictographs and petroglyphs on the rock walls—evidence of human occupancy in this region that dates back more than 11,500 years. Located 35 miles south of Klamath Falls off Hwy. 139.

The striking geological features of California's Lava Beds National Monument are the work of thousands of years of volcanic action.

③ LAKE TAHOE, CALIFORNIA/NEVADA

Described by Mark Twain as "the fairest picture the whole earth affords," Lake Tahoe is an inland sea ringed by the peaks of the Sierra Nevada. This beguiling azure lake is situated 6,223 feet above sea level. The Washoe Indians thought the lake was bottomless. In fact, Lake Tahoe is 1,645 feet deep, ranking as the tenth-deepest lake in North America. A 72-mile-long scenic road allows visitors to sample shoreline attractions such as Zephyr Cove, Meeks Bay, Tahoe City, Kings Beach, and Emerald Bay State Park. A U.S. Forest Service visitor center provides interpretive programs on the flora and fauna and is the starting point for several self-guided walking trails. Located on Hwy 50.

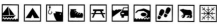

④ ARMSTRONG REDWOODS STATE RESERVE, CALIFORNIA

Home to some of the oldest redwood trees in the world, this 728-acre reserve is a living museum of Northern California's natural history. A self-guided walking trail winds through groves of coastal redwoods, which can grow more than 350 feet high and live up to 2,000 years. The Parson Jones Tree—the tallest redwood in the reserve—soars to 310 feet, making it 3 feet taller than the Statue of Liberty. Tanbark oaks, bracken ferns, big leaf maples, and California laurels also thrive in the forest. The grove was owned in the 1870's by lumberman Col. James Armstrong, whose efforts ultimately led to its preservation as a unit of the California state park system. Located 2½ miles north of the town of Guerneville on Armstrong Woods Rd.

⑤ SEA LION CAVES, OREGON

Higher than a 12-story building and longer than a football field, this massive cave harbors Steller and California sea lions. An elevator, descending 208 feet to sea level, provides easy access to this multihued natural amphitheater. As many as 200 sea lions congregate here during the fall and winter months; in the spring and summer, they breed and give birth on rocky ledges just outside the cave. Gulls, Brandt's cormorants, and pigeon guillemots can be spotted here during their nesting periods. Located 11 miles north of Florence on Hwy. 101.

⑥ FORT CLATSOP NATIONAL MEMORIAL, OREGON

When Meriwether Lewis and William Clark reached the Pacific Ocean near the end of their expedition of 1804-06, they built a small fort to serve as their winter quarters. Today the 50-foot fort includes stockaded quarters, a guard room, and a storeroom. Reconstruction work was based on etchings from Clark's field book. During the summer, costumed interpreters demonstrate day-to-day activities of the fort. Located 5 miles south of Astoria off Hwy 101.

⑦ GRAYS HARBOR HISTORICAL SEAPORT, WASHINGTON

A former shipyard and lumber mill, Grays Harbor is now a maritime museum with a full-scale operational replica of the 18th-century sailing vessel *Lady Washington*. Constructed from old-growth Douglas fir, the ship is 112 feet long, with an 89-foot mast, and was the largest fully square-rigged sailing ship to ply the West Coast. Visitors can tour the vessel; the seaport also offers sailing courses aboard *Lady Washington*. Located in the town of Aberdeen.

Set amid the splendor of the Sierra Nevada and the Carson Range, Lake Tahoe is 12 miles wide, 22 miles long, and contains almost 40 trillion gallons of water.

THE ROYAL ROUTE

*Isolated in the balmy Pacific, the
Hawaiian Islands gave birth to
a larger-than-life royal dynasty.*

When their epic voyages of discovery brought the ancient Polynesian explorers across the Pacific Ocean to the Hawaiian Islands soon after the birth of Christ, they found unique flora and fauna, majestic mountains, sandy shores, deep valleys streaming with waterfalls, and cloud-wreathed rain forests. These first Hawaiians developed a culture that was finely attuned to the natural beauty around them and told their stories through the swaying grace of the hula—a dance whose every gesture, every glance is invested with nuance.

For centuries, the Hawaiians—farther from any land mass than any other people on earth— were alone beneath the brilliant oceanic stars that had guided them on their wanderings. Although the islanders produced the finest flowering of Polynesian art and culture, conflict often flared between tribes and clans. Out of this constant fcuding emerged a king, Kamehameha I, also known as Kamehameha the Great, who united the islands in 1810 and founded a royal dynasty

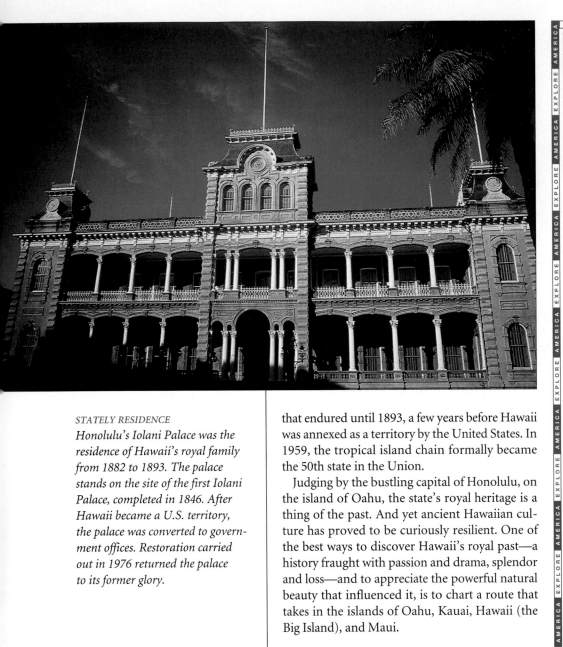

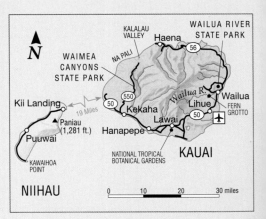

STATELY RESIDENCE
Honolulu's Iolani Palace was the residence of Hawaii's royal family from 1882 to 1893. The palace stands on the site of the first Iolani Palace, completed in 1846. After Hawaii became a U.S. territory, the palace was converted to government offices. Restoration carried out in 1976 returned the palace to its former glory.

GARDEN COAST
Overleaf: On Kauai's spectacular Na Pali coast, tropical vegetation clings to rugged cliffs that plunge straight into the Pacific Ocean.

that endured until 1893, a few years before Hawaii was annexed as a territory by the United States. In 1959, the tropical island chain formally became the 50th state in the Union.

Judging by the bustling capital of Honolulu, on the island of Oahu, the state's royal heritage is a thing of the past. And yet ancient Hawaiian culture has proved to be curiously resilient. One of the best ways to discover Hawaii's royal past—a history fraught with passion and drama, splendor and loss—and to appreciate the powerful natural beauty that influenced it, is to chart a route that takes in the islands of Oahu, Kauai, Hawaii (the Big Island), and Maui.

HONOLULU'S
PALACE

The place to begin retracing America's only royal dynasty is Iolani Palace, located in the heart of Honolulu. From 1882 to 1893, the palace was the residence of the royal family. Ironically, this is also the place where Kamehameha's dynasty came to an end. The last royal event here was a grand luau given on November 16, 1892. Three days later, in the palace's Blue Room, Hawaii's last queen—Liliuokalani—was forced to surrender the kingdom of Hawaii to Sanford Dole, the son of American missionaries who came to the islands in the early 1800's. Dole became the president of the newly formed republic and its governor when Hawaii was annexed into the United States by President McKinley in 1898.

Rebuilt in 1883, Iolani Palace now sits amid a broad green lawn with gleaming business towers

SEASIDE FLORA
The striking orange petals of the lobster claw heliconia bear a remarkable resemblance to certain denizens of the islands' coral reefs.

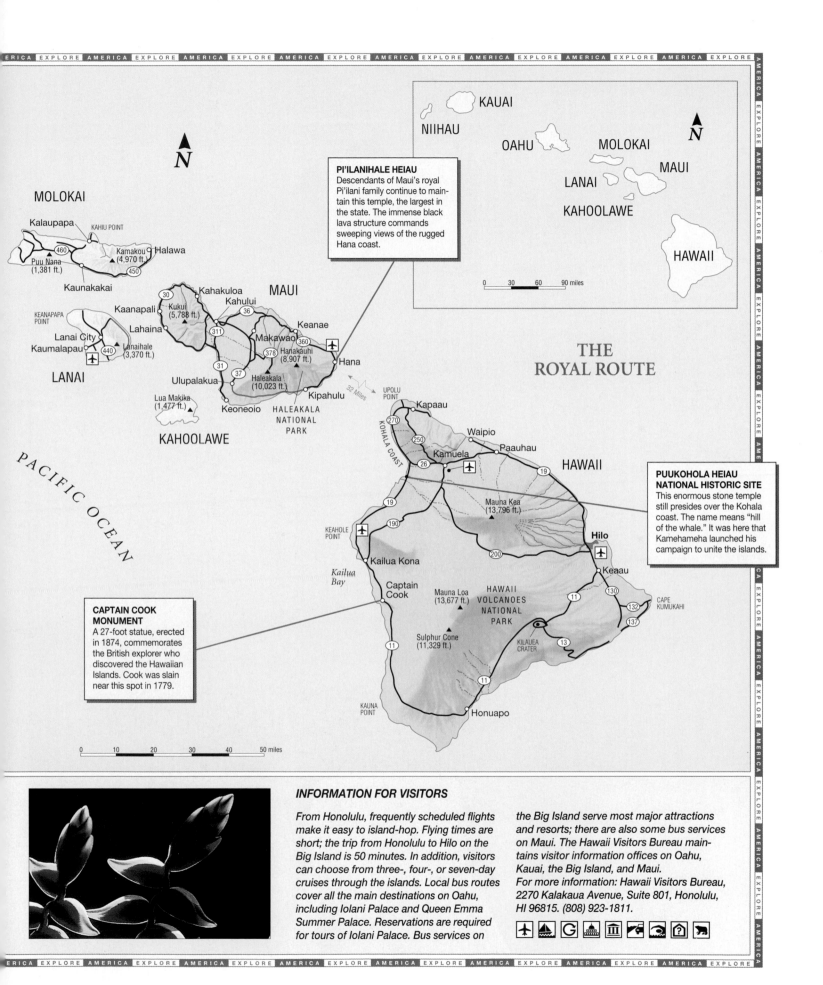

KAUAI

NIIHAU

OAHU   MOLOKAI

LANAI   MAUI

KAHOOLAWE

HAWAII

0   30   60   90 miles

MOLOKAI

Kalaupapa
KAHIU POINT
Puu Nana   Kamakou   •Halawa
(1,381 ft.)   (4,970 ft.)
460   450
Kaunakakai

KEANAPAPA
POINT

Lanai City
Kaumalapau   Lanaihale
440   (3,370 ft.)

LANAI

PI'ILANIHALE HEIAU
Descendants of Maui's royal
Pi'ilani family continue to maintain this temple, the largest in
the state. The immense black
lava structure commands
sweeping views of the rugged
Hana coast.

MAUI

Kahakuloa
30   Kahului
Kaanapali   Kukui
(5,788 ft.)   36
Kaanapali
311   Makawao
Lahaina   Keanae
360
378   Hanakauhi
31   (8,907 ft.)
37   Hana
Ulupalakua
Haleakala
Lua Makika   (10,023 ft.)
(1,477 ft.)   Keoneoio   Kipahulu
HALEAKALA
NATIONAL
KAHOOLAWE   PARK

32 Miles

THE
ROYAL ROUTE

UPOLU
POINT
Kapaau

270
KOHALA COAST
250   Waipio
26   Kamuela   Paauhau
HAWAII
19

19   Mauna Kea
(13,796 ft.)
KEAHOLE
POINT   190
Hilo
200
Kailua Kona
Keaau
Kailua
Bay   Captain   Mauna Loa   HAWAII   11   130
Cook   (13,677 ft.)   VOLCANOES   CAPE
NATIONAL   132   KUMUKAHI
PARK   137
Sulphur Cone
(11,329 ft.)   KILAUEA
11   CRATER   13

CAPTAIN COOK
MONUMENT
A 27-foot statue, erected
in 1874, commemorates
the British explorer who
discovered the Hawaiian
Islands. Cook was slain
near this spot in 1779.

PUUKOHOLA HEIAU
NATIONAL HISTORIC SITE
This enormous stone temple
still presides over the Kohala
coast. The name means "hill
of the whale." It was here that
Kamehameha launched his
campaign to unite the islands.

KAUNA
POINT   Honuapo

PACIFIC OCEAN

0   10   20   30   40   50 miles

INFORMATION FOR VISITORS

*From Honolulu, frequently scheduled flights
make it easy to island-hop. Flying times are
short; the trip from Honolulu to Hilo on the
Big Island is 50 minutes. In addition, visitors
can choose from three-, four-, or seven-day
cruises through the islands. Local bus routes
cover all the main destinations on Oahu,
including Iolani Palace and Queen Emma
Summer Palace. Reservations are required
for tours of Iolani Palace. Bus services on*
*the Big Island serve most major attractions
and resorts; there are also some bus services
on Maui. The Hawaii Visitors Bureau maintains visitor information offices on Oahu,
Kauai, the Big Island, and Maui.
For more information: Hawaii Visitors Bureau,
2270 Kalakaua Avenue, Suite 801, Honolulu,
HI 96815. (808) 923-1811.*

ERICA EXPLORE AMERICA EXPLORE AMERICA EXPLORE AMERICA EXPLORE AMERICA EXPLORE AMERICA EXPLORE AMERICA EXPLORE AMERICA EXPLORE AMERICA EXPLORE

THE ROYAL ROUTE 97

rising around it. On Fridays, office workers sit on the grass and listen to concerts by the Royal Hawaiian Band in the coronation gazebo. Now open to the public, Iolani Palace symbolizes a revival of interest in Hawaii's royal past. Its Florentine Renaissance architecture incorporates Victorian flourishes and wide Hawaiian lanais, or verandas. The beautifully restored interior rooms glow in fine native hardwoods: koa, kamani, kou, and ohia. The red-and-gold throne room is lit by crystal chandeliers. The dining room is once again set for dinner with porcelain china, made in Paris, bearing the Hawaiian coat of arms. The silverware was a gift from Emperor Napoleon III; the crystal is Bohemian.

In their heyday, Hawaii's kings and queens would retreat from the heat of Honolulu to the cool uplands of Oahu. Along the Pali Highway, King Kamehameha IV and his wife, Queen Emma, spent their summers in a gracious white home, which was prefabricated in Boston and shipped around Cape Horn to the island in 1847. Bequeathed to the royal family in 1857, the house is now a museum called the Queen Emma Summer Palace. Every room contains royal treasures and exquisite Victorian furniture. Of particular note is the canoe-shaped cradle of their son, who died tragically at the age of four.

The Pali Highway continues to climb into the green reaches of the Koolau Mountains, where waterfalls tumble on both sides of the road. The highway leads to one of the most famous battle sites in Hawaii as well as one of the most beautiful panoramas in all the world: Two hundred years ago, at Nuuanu Pali Lookout, warriors defending Oahu were driven over the sheer cliffs to their deaths by the army of Kamehameha I during his campaign to unite the Hawaiian islands. Today emerald mountain ramparts plunge in saw-toothed palisades, and the windward coast spreads out in a glory of sea and sky.

GARDEN ISLAND

Of Hawaii's six main islands, the only one not conquered by Kamehameha I was Kauai, although he mounted two ill-fated seaborne campaigns against it. Eventually, though, Kauai's last king, Kaumualii, bowed to the inevitable and placed his island domain under Kamehameha's flag. Kauai—also known as the Garden Island—is a lot easier to get to today than it was for Kamehameha, and the island retains tantalizing reminders of its royal history.

King Kaumualii was born at the royal birthing place—a group of black lava rocks reputed to embody spiritual strength—in a district along the Wailua River, Hawaii's only navigable watercourse, known in those days as *Wailua Nui Hoano* or Great Sacred Wailua. The area's significance dates to the earliest days of Polynesian settlement. The birthing stones and the ruins of an ancient lava rock temple where human sacrifice was practiced lie near Wailua River State Park. The black sacrificial stones are now softened by lichen lace. Today, kayakers use the park as a starting point to explore the river. In the days of the Hawaiian kings, a series of temples stood sentinel on the banks, and priests and nobility lived in a royal village surrounded by patches of taro—a food crop that is common to the Pacific islands—and fish ponds.

The Wailua River trickles down from the green heart of Kauai, then divides into fingers, finally broadening at its mouth. Hau trees form a canopy and drop golden flowers into the river's jade-green waters. Towering waterfalls are fed by streams that rush from Mount Waialeale, the wettest spot on earth with a soggy 40 feet of rain a year. Kayakers can almost always count on a shower even when the sun is shining along the shore, blazing into rainbows so broad they become curtains of color.

FERNS AND FLUTED CLIFFS
Amau ferns blanket the slopes of the Kalalau Valley, opposite page, on Kauai's north shore.

WARRIOR KING
Hung with garlands, a bronze statue of King Kamehameha I, left, presides over downtown Honolulu. The statue is actually a cast of the original, which was lost off the Falkland Islands while in transit to Hawaii. After a duplicate was ordered for Honolulu, the original statue was salvaged and placed in Kapaau, on the Big Island.

FIT FOR A QUEEN
A gracious pillared porch greets visitors to the Queen Emma Summer Palace, below. The modest yet elegant royal retreat is located in the hills outside Honolulu.

The rugged coastal scenery of Kauai defies civilization—there is no road that goes all around the island—so a boat or helicopter is the preferred means of travel. The 11-mile-long Kalalau Trail provides hikers with a close-up look at the spectacular scenery of coastline. Where Kuhio Highway (Route 56) ends in Haena, the grandeur of the Na Pali coast begins. For 20 miles, volcanic cliffs, hanging valleys, and feathery waterfalls unfold along one of the world's greatest scenic coasts. At the base of the green fluted cliffs is Ke'e beach and its barrier reef, where snorkelers swim among coral canyons teeming with schools of spangled tropical fish. Just above the beach is a ruined hula temple. Dancers still come to offer homage to the gods and to test their voices against the roar of the surf, where the ocean is so powerful that the land actually trembles under the onslaught. One classic Hawaiian tale unfolded at the temple when Pele, goddess of volcanoes, fell in love with a handsome king of Kauai. The tempestuous deity finally consumed the monarch. All that is left of the temple are lava stones, some low walls, and grassy areas that once echoed with the tread of hundreds of dancers.

During the 1870's, Queen Emma also savored the ethereal beauty of Kauai. After the death of her husband and her only child, the queen retreated to lands she had inherited at Lawaii, and there gave herself over to her passion for gardening. She planted laua'e ferns, ginger, heliconia, orchids, rose apple, bamboo, pandanus, haole lehua, pikake, and spider lily, as well as such trees as tamarind, thornless kiawe, kamani, and mango. The brilliant magenta bougainvillea that cascade over the Lawaii cliffs today grew from slips planted by Emma. In rough clothes, with hat, veil, and gloves, the queen worked along with her gardeners to give the land new life.

Subsequent owners developed water gardens and incorporated a wider variety of tropical flora. In 1964 the 186-acre estate—which boasts more than 6,000 species of tropical plants—was chartered by Congress as the National Tropical Botanical Gardens. It then became part of the Pacific Tropical Botanical Garden in 1971. Botanical and horticultural research and education are conducted at the site, which is open for public tours.

From the air, it is clear why the island of Hawaii is known as the Big Island: it is twice as large as all the others combined. It is apparent, too, that this is the true home of Pele—the airport runways are hacked out of lava and volcanoes dominate the skyline. One of these, Mauna Kea, is so high that its

RIGHTEOUS MOTTO
The coat of arms of the Hawaiian kingdom, mounted on the gate of the royal mausoleum at Nuuanu, on Oahu, bears a motto that translates as "the life of the land is perpetuated in righteousness."

RIVER ROAD
Tour boats cruise Kauai's Wailua River to the natural wonder of Fern Grotto, a cavern filled with luxuriant ferns. Along the way, hula dancers and storytellers recount Hawaii's royal history, as they have done for generations.

summit is covered in snow for much of the year. Skiers can slalom all day and return to the shore to watch the sunset under swaying palm trees.

The king who would unite the islands was born on the Big Island. Legend has it that on a night in 1753, as a comet streaked across the dark oceanic skies, a Hawaiian princess gave birth to a son near the northern tip of the island. She cradled her baby in her arms before retainers took him to a nearby temple for his birth rituals. Haste was necessary, for the ruling chief of the island, fearing a child born under such omens, had ordered the infant's death. That very night, mother and son were spirited away and hidden in the Waipio Valley. The child was named Kamehameha, later to rule the islands as Kamehameha I. Waipio Valley was a fitting home for a future king: it had been the seat of a long succession of Big Island rulers, beginning in the early 1300's and ending when the court was moved to Kona in 1600. From the valley overlook today, the Waipio Valley is quilted in taro farms and hemmed by a black sand beach with foaming white surf. The walls of the valley tower more than 2,000 feet in height.

After his military successes, Kamehameha I proved to be as wise in peace as he was fierce in warfare. He retired in 1812 to a royal compound along the shores of his home island at Kailua Bay, where he built the temple of Ahuena Heiau. Unlike most other temples in Hawaii, this one has been faithfully restored. Its grass structures, prayer oracle, and ki'i god images once again watch over the mouth of Kailua Bay on the grounds of the Hotel King Kamehameha.

Across the water, in the town of Kailua Kona, is a later, grander royal residence—Hulihe'e Palace. When it was completed in 1838, a local newspaper called it "the most splendid building at the Sandwich Islands." In 1925 it became a museum. Inside are many of the original furnishings, including a four-poster bed from Kamehameha I's grass palace and a table inlaid with 20 varieties of Hawaiian hardwood. The furniture is enormous, built to accommodate the physical stature of the *ali'i* (nobility). Judging by the length of his spear, which stands in the stairwell, Kamehameha must have stood seven feet tall.

All along the coast of the Big Island, remnants of royalty are scattered among the resorts. On the greens of the Keauhou-Kona golf course there stands a royal *holua*, a stone ramp thatched with ti and banana leaves that was used for a tropical version of sledding. A temple dedicated to surfing—for centuries a favorite sport of the Hawaiians—shares holy ground with a Roman Catholic church. The Keauhou Beach Hotel has preserved a royal beach house and an ancient aquaculture pond, where fish were raised for the tables of the chiefs.

Although Hawaii's royal saga may have begun on the Big Island, the first official capital of the Hawaiian kingdom was located at Lahaina, on the island of Maui. There the royal family lived in languid splendor in a residence located on an island in the middle of a lake. Today the lake is gone and this sacred site lies buried under Lahaina's softball field. What has survived the ravages of time, however, is Lahaina's distinct Yankee flavor, for the town gained notoriety as a favorite port of call for explorers and the American whaling fleet during the early 1800's. Kings, queens, and missionaries intent on saving souls were arrayed against the unruly sailors, who maintained there was no God west of Cape Horn and behaved accordingly. The town's former grog shops and ships' chandlers are now art galleries and restaurants, and once-tottering old buildings have been renovated and are now very fashionable.

Hawaii's royal family would retreat to Kaanapali, on the west coast of Maui, for rest, swimming, surfing, and luaus that lasted for weeks. The hotels that are now scattered along the perfect crescent beach offer much the same thing today. At Kaanapali, the royal route becomes a red carpet for the new monarch of the islands—the visitor.

Everywhere in the islands, Hawaii's royal heritage lives on. Amid the luxuriant natural beauty, the temples, palaces, and shrines serve as persistent reminders of a lost kingdom that seems to grow stronger, dearer, with the passage of time.

MEETING GROUND
Canoes beached beside the restored temple of Ahuena Heiau, above, on the island of Hawaii, are a reminder of the seafaring heritage of the Hawaiian people. King Kamehameha I conducted government meetings on the grounds of this temple, which was dedicated to the arts, healing, and fertility.

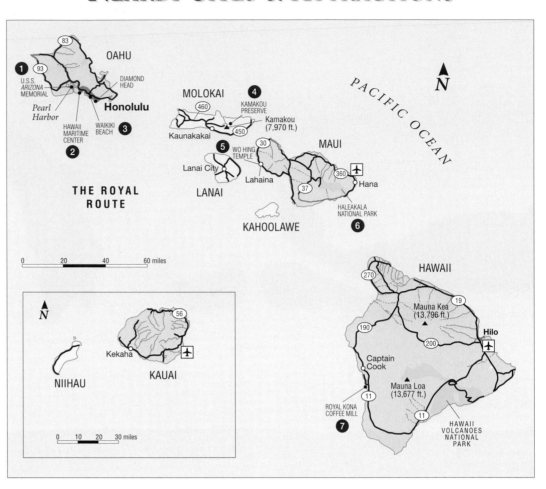

Hawaii's state bird, the endangered nene, makes its home in Haleakala National Park, on the island of Maui. Once on the brink of extinction, the nene has recovered thanks to a captive breeding program begun in England during the 1950's.

① U.S.S. *ARIZONA* MEMORIAL, OAHU

A stark white monument moored in Pearl Harbor marks the resting place of the U.S.S. *Arizona*, which exploded and sank during the Japanese attack on Pearl Harbor on December 7, 1941. Of the 2,404 Americans who were killed, 1,177 were part of the crew of the U.S.S. *Arizona*; the remains of 1,102 sailors are entombed in the ship. At the memorial's visitor center, a film depicting the attack is shown; visitors then take a boat to the memorial. The names of the deceased are inscribed on the walls of the shrine room. The visitor center is on Pearl Harbor Navy Base off Hwy. 99 (Kamehameha Highway).

② HAWAII MARITIME CENTER, OAHU

This museum explores Hawaii's maritime history. Displays chart the epic ocean voyages of Polynesian navigators and boat builders, Captain James Cook's discovery of the islands in 1778, the history of surfing, and Hawaii's many shipwrecks. The center's most popular attractions are the *Hokulea*, a reconstructed double-hulled canoe used by the Polynesian navigators, and the restored sailing ship *Falls of Clyde*, the last four-masted square-rigger in the world. Located at Pier 7 in Honolulu Harbor.

③ WAIKIKI BEACH, OAHU

One of the world's most famous surfing beaches, Waikiki Beach is both a modern city suburb and an exotic tropical paradise. The two-mile-long strip of sand attracts 100,000 visitors a day and is separated from Honolulu by the Ala Wai Canal, built in 1922 to drain the once-swampy area. When Captain Cook and his crew sailed past the beach in 1778, they were impressed at the skillful way in which Hawaiians used planks of wood from native koa and wili-wili trees to ride the waves. Since then, surfers have taken advantage of its spectacular surf. Located in Honolulu.

④ KAMAKOU PRESERVE, MOLOKAI

The rugged 2,744-acre preserve, accessible only by four-wheel-drive vehicle, protects some of Molokai's most important natural habitats, ranging from dry lowland forests and shrublands to the lush rain forest that cloaks the summit of Mount Kamakou, a 4,970-foot volcanic dome that is the island's highest peak. From Waikolu Lookout, a picnic area at the top of the access road, visitors can enjoy stunning views of the surrounding area and the Pacific Ocean. Scheduled hikes offer a chance to see a variety of native birds, including the amakihi and apapane, both members of the honeycreeper family. The apapane's bright red feathers were once used by Hawaiians to make royal cloaks. Of the area's 250 species of plants, some 219 are found only in the Hawaiian Islands. Located on the Forest Reserve Jeep Road east of Hwy. 46.

⑤ WO HING TEMPLE, MAUI

Hawaii's Chinese population dates from 1788, when the first Chinese laborers arrived to work on the islands' sugar plantations. Their legacy is celebrated in this museum, housed in a traditional Buddhist temple. Built in 1912, the temple was originally intended to teach Chinese social values to the younger generation and to maintain links between Maui's older Chinese population and their homeland. The museum also includes the original temple cookhouse, a Buddhist shrine, and a theater exhibiting films on Chinese Hawaiian history, including two films made by Thomas Edison in 1898 and 1906. Located on Front Street in Lahaina.

⑥ HALEAKALA NATIONAL PARK, MAUI

The gigantic cone of Mount Haleakala—the world's largest dormant volcano—dominates Haleakala National Park, the third-smallest of the national parks. Designated an International Biosphere Reserve by the United Nations, the 29,000-acre park preserves the fragile ecosystem that extends from the volcanic highlands down to the rugged Kipahulu coast. The immense volcano is up to 3,000 feet deep and 19 square miles in area. Only the western rim is accessible by road; the rest of the park must be seen on foot or on horseback. Haleakala is home to the endangered silversword, which flowers only once before it dies. The park is also prime nesting territory for the nene, the native Hawaiian goose. To protect the park environment, the Kipahulu Valley is closed to the public. Coastal trails wind through

forests of ginger, kukui, and mango. Hwys. 37, 377, and 378 lead to Haleakala summit; Hwys. 36 and 360 lead to the coastal section of the park.

⑦ ROYAL KONA COFFEE MILL, HAWAII

Hawaii is the only state in the United States to grow coffee commercially, and its Kona coffee is world-renowned. The rich volcanic soil on the western slopes of Mauna Loa has been used to grow coffee since 1820, when missionaries planted the first bean. Today, annual production tops 2.4 million pounds. The mill and museum tell the story of the birth of Kona coffee and offer the chance to sample the rich brew. Visitors can also walk through the coffee orchards' elevated slopes. Located 4 miles south of the town of Captain Cook on Hwy. 11.

Dedicated in 1962, the U.S.S. Arizona Memorial in Pearl Harbor spans the middle portion of the sunken battleship. In a special tribute to the ship and its lost crew, the Stars and Stripes flies from a pole attached to the Arizona's original mainmast.

With the volcanic bulk of Diamond Head rising at its southeastern end, Waikiki Beach is one of Hawaii's most popular vacation destinations.

THE INSIDE PASSAGE

Shaped by glaciers, southeastern Alaska is a rugged maze of islands where nature reigns supreme.

Naturalist John Muir wrote of Alaska's Inside Passage: "Were the attractions of this north coast half known, thousands of lovers of nature's beauties would come hither every year. I know of no excursion in any part of our vast country where so much is unfolded in so short a time." And hither they come every year indeed: by cruise ship, state ferry, float plane, fishing boat, sailboat, even sea kayak to see the temperate rain forests, tidewater glaciers, nautical hamlets, and ethnically diverse faces of southeastern Alaska; to see eagles and bears, seals and whales; to smell the salt air and taste the adventure of that famous marine highway called the Inside Passage.

"Where the road ends, the real Alaska begins," say locals in Alaska. The roads of the Inside Passage are not roads at all; they're fjords, canals, straits, inlets, coves, and bays. More than a thousand islands punctuate this coast, most of them verdant with Sitka spruce, western hemlock, and western red cedar. The green, shaggy slopes of the mainland climb into clouds where glaciers

ICE SCULPTURES
Originally part of McBride Glacier in Glacier Bay National Park, these iceberg fragments have been melted into fantastic shapes by the warmth of the sun.

BLOOMING SHORE
Overleaf: Overshadowed by the snowcapped mountains in the background, dainty dwarf fireweed flourishes along the shore of the western arm of Glacier Bay. As the glacier slowly retreats, pioneering plant life revitalizes the soil.

spill down from ice-mantled peaks and white, sealike icefields.

The rain can fall steadily for weeks at a time—hundreds of inches a year in some places. This is soggy, roadless country, where history and geography have conspired to make every furrow and hollow a world unto itself. Those who call it home like it that way.

The southeastern Alaska panhandle reaches down from central Alaska toward the Pacific Northwest of the contiguous United States. Four hundred miles long and roughly 125 miles wide, the panhandle is flanked by the Coast Mountains and the U.S.–Canada International Boundary to the east and the Pacific Ocean to the west. Fierce winter storms rake the outer, western coasts of Yakobi, Kruzof, Baranof, Prince of Wales, and Dall islands, while calmer waters prevail inside on the leeward shores. This is the Inside Passage, notable not only for its spectacular scenery and wildlife but also for its relatively protected waters and smooth sailing.

Journeys usually begin from Seattle or Bellingham in Washington State, or from Vancouver in British Columbia, and go more than 1,000 miles to Haines and Skagway, once the gateway to the Klondike goldfield. Travelers sail along the wild British Columbia coast, past the Queen Charlotte Islands—home of the Haidas, master carvers of totem poles and canoes. Then comes Dixon Entrance, exposed to the open Pacific, followed by Clarence Strait and Tongass Narrows. The first port of call in Alaska's Inside Passage is Ketchikan.

Built on the dual industries of fishing and timber, Ketchikan is a roll-up-your-sleeves working town of about 14,000, where seaside homes stand on wooden pilings above high tide and boats of all

INFORMATION FOR VISITORS

Several cruise lines offer extensive tours of the Inside Passage from May through September. The Alaska state ferry system provides year-round service to Ketchikan, Wrangell, Petersburg, Sitka, Juneau, Haines, and Skagway. Smaller ferries serve some of the other towns and villages in the region. Commercial air service is available to Juneau, Ketchikan, Sitka, Petersburg, and Wrangell. Several smaller air carriers connect many of the towns of the Inside Passage. Three highways traverse southeastern Alaska: the Alaska Highway, the Haines Highway, and the Klondike Highway. The White Pass & Yukon narrow-gauge railroad travels from Fraser, British Columbia, to Skagway, Alaska.
For more information: Southeast Alaska Tourism Council, P.O. Box 20710, Juneau, AK 99802-0710. (907) 586-4777.

STUDY IN VERSATILITY
A horned puffin enjoys a restful moment amid a sea of grass. These adaptable seabirds use their wings to swim as well as to fly.

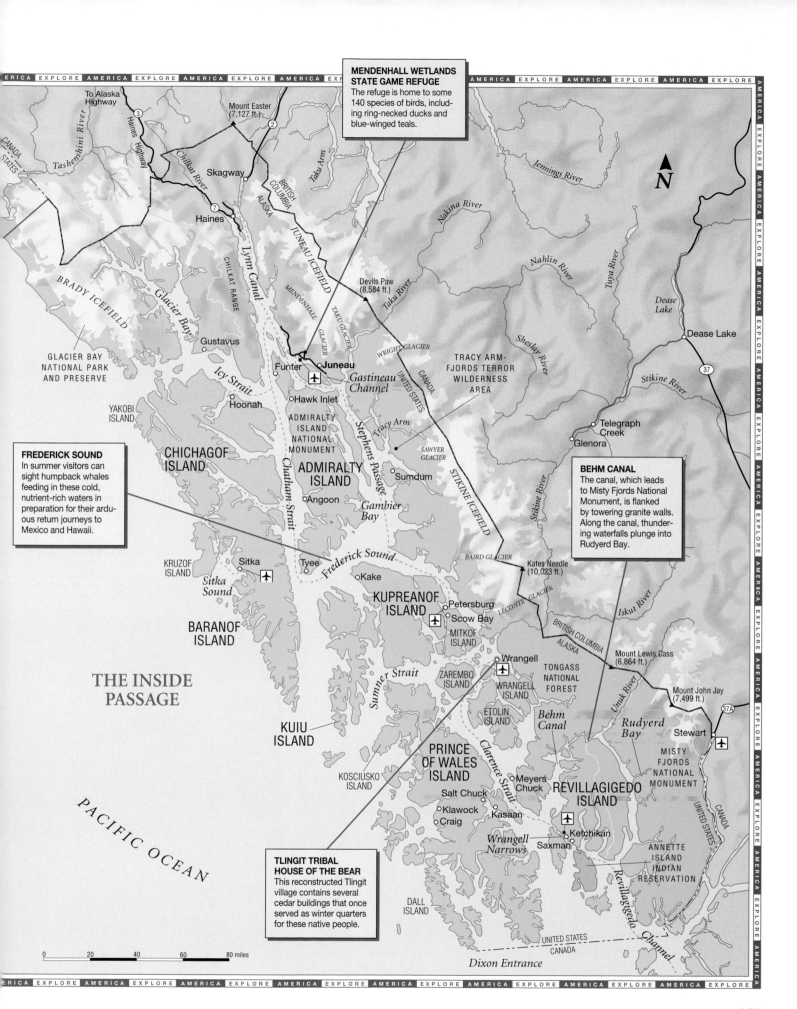

MENDENHALL WETLANDS STATE GAME REFUGE
The refuge is home to some 140 species of birds, including ring-necked ducks and blue-winged teals.

To Alaska Highway

Mount Easter
(7,127 ft.)

3

2

Haines Highway

Skagway

Jennings River

N

Tashenshini River

Chilkat River

7

Haines

BRITISH COLUMBIA

ALASKA

Taku Arm

Nakina River

CHILKAT RANGE

Lynn Canal

JUNEAU ICEFIELD

Nahlin River

Tuya River

Dease Lake

BRADY ICEFIELD

MENDENHALL GLACIER

TAKU GLACIER

Devils Paw
(8,584 ft.)

Taku River

Sheslay River

Dease Lake

37

Glacier Bay

Gustavus

Funter

Juneau

WRIGHT GLACIER

Stikine River

GLACIER BAY NATIONAL PARK AND PRESERVE

Icy Strait

Gastineau Channel

UNITED STATES

CANADA

Telegraph Creek

YAKOBI ISLAND

Hoonah

Hawk Inlet

Stephens Passage

Tracy Arm

TRACY ARM-FJORDS TERROR WILDERNESS AREA

Glenora

FREDERICK SOUND
In summer visitors can sight humpback whales feeding in these cold, nutrient-rich waters in preparation for their arduous return journeys to Mexico and Hawaii.

CHICHAGOF ISLAND

ADMIRALTY ISLAND NATIONAL MONUMENT

ADMIRALTY ISLAND

Sawyer Glacier

Sumdum

SAWYER GLACIER

STIKINE ICEFIELD

BEHM CANAL
The canal, which leads to Misty Fjords National Monument, is flanked by towering granite walls. Along the canal, thundering waterfalls plunge into Rudyerd Bay.

Angoon

Gambier Bay

Stikine River

KRUZOF ISLAND

Sitka

Tyee

Frederick Sound

Kake

BAIRD GLACIER

Kates Needle
(10,023 ft.)

Sitka Sound

Chatham Strait

LECONTE GLACIER

BARANOF ISLAND

KUPREANOF ISLAND

Petersburg

Scow Bay

MITKOF ISLAND

Iskut River

BRITISH COLUMBIA

ALASKA

Mount Lewis Cass
(6,864 ft.)

THE INSIDE PASSAGE

Summer Strait

ZAREMBO ISLAND

Wrangell

TONGASS NATIONAL FOREST

WRANGELL ISLAND

Unuk River

Mount John Jay
(7,499 ft.)

37A

KUIU ISLAND

ETOLIN ISLAND

Behm Canal

Rudyerd Bay

Stewart

Clarence Strait

PRINCE OF WALES ISLAND

KOSCIUSKO ISLAND

Meyers Chuck

Behm Canal

MISTY FJORDS NATIONAL MONUMENT

REVILLAGIGEDO ISLAND

PACIFIC OCEAN

Salt Chuck

Klawock

Kasaan

Craig

TLINGIT TRIBAL HOUSE OF THE BEAR
This reconstructed Tlingit village contains several cedar buildings that once served as winter quarters for these native people.

Wrangell Narrows

Ketchikan

Saxman

ANNETTE ISLAND INDIAN RESERVATION

Revillagigedo Channel

DALL ISLAND

UNITED STATES

CANADA

Dixon Entrance

0   20   40   60   80 miles

manner fill the harbor. Known as the Salmon Capital of the World, Ketchikan owes much of its wealth to all five species of Pacific salmon— king, silver, red, humpback, and chum—which every year return from the open sea to swim the rivers and streams of southeastern Alaska.

Just east of Ketchikan, the tendril-like fingers of Misty Fjords National Monument reach deep into forested slopes beneath sheer granite walls thousands of feet high, many of them resplendent with tumbling waterfalls.

PRINCE OF WALES ISLAND The northward journey passes along the eastern shore of Prince of Wales Island. With an area of 2,731 square miles, this is the largest island in the Inside Passage and the center of a complex of literally hundreds of small rocky islets. Once completely blanketed in a rich tapestry of centuries-old spruces, hemlocks, and cedars, major portions of Prince of Wales Island have been intensively logged, with much of the raw wood going to Asia for use by the construction and rayon industries. A significant portion of the southern end of the island is protected wilderness, and a healthy population of wolves lives here.

On Admiralty Island to the north, black and brown bears are abundant, but seeing these animals from the deck of a ship or a boat isn't easy. They are secretive and shy, and the thick vegetation camouflages them.

Bald eagles typically perch and build their nests in conifers along the shores of the Inside Passage and can be seen easily as the white heads of the adults make a striking contrast against the dark vegetation. An estimated 10,000 adult bald eagles live in southeastern Alaska—roughly the same number believed to have lived in the area prior to settlement by Europeans.

A short passage north of Ketchikan brings the traveler to the frontier-spirited towns of Wrangell and Petersburg. Just south of Petersburg, between Mitkof and Kupreanof islands, is Wrangell Narrows, the most famous stretch of water along the whole of the Inside Passage. Winding like a ribbon for 21 miles, narrowing at one point to only 100 yards' width, the narrows beckons all passengers on deck to view the shoreline trees that seem close enough to touch. Large cruise ships do not pass through here, but the Alaska State Ferries—a fleet of boats affectionately called the Blue Canoes—make regular runs. Tidal currents as strong as eight knots rip through the narrows, which is punctuated with so many red and green navigational lights that Alaskans have dubbed it Christmas Tree Lane.

Petersburg was founded in 1897 by Norwegian fishermen Peter Bushman, who also started the town's fish cannery. Hospitable Petersburg boasts a rich Scandinavian heritage. Some of the town's streets are still planked with wood, and the homes, built on stilts above the high tide level, stand in respectful salutation to the sea.

TOWERS OF ICE

Located only 25 miles east of Petersburg is the LeConte Glacier, the most southerly tidewater glacier in North America. The LeConte spills downslope from the Stikine Icefield, and by the time the glacier gets to sea level—its hypnotic blue face towering some 200 feet out of the water—great fins and towers of ice stand at precarious angles, ready to fall. Travelers take a collective deep breath and wait expectantly for the glacier to crack.

A massive shard of ice peels away from the terminus, seemingly in slow motion at first, and then rapidly plummets downward and hits the sea with a sound the native Tlingit called "White Thunder."

The shard fractures into icebergs that slowly drift away with the tides. Harbor seals crawl onto them to rest. Mother seals even give birth to their pups on the icebergs, where they find safety from predators on land and in the sea (the latter primarily being orcas, or killer whales).

A short distance north of Petersburg and the LeConte Glacier, the Inside Passage opens into Frederick Sound—one of the best places in the state to see humpback whales. After a winter in the warmer waters of Hawaii and Mexico, where they give birth to their calves and eat very little, the gentle but hungry humpbacks return every summer to the waters of the Inside Passage, where they gorge

FREE RIDE
A killer whale calf hitches a ride on the back of its mother. Full-grown orcas average 23 feet in length and weigh about nine tons. They are easily identified by their distinctive black-and-white markings and usually travel in groups.

on herring, capelin, sand lance, and other small fish that flourish in the cold waters. It's a thrill to suddenly see an adult humpback—which can grow up to 45 feet long and weigh 40 tons—spouting on the horizon, flapping its 15-foot-long flippers, lobbing its tail, or leaping completely out of the sea in a full-body breach.

Most journeys through the Inside Passage make a foray along the west coast of Baranof Island to the town of Sitka, nestled in a picturesque and protected harbor where Tlingit Indians first settled more than 9,000 years ago. In 1741 Russian explorers probed along the coast, collecting samples of the region's wealth of fur-bearing animals. In 1799 a Russian expedition under Alexander Baranov

RIVERSIDE REPOSE
A brown bear and her two cubs bask on the banks of a coastal river. Also known as the coastal brown bear or the grizzly, the brown bear has a distinctive hump over its shoulders that distinguishes it from the black bear. A mature brown male weighs between 500 and 900 pounds. As many as 8,000 brown bears inhabit southeastern Alaska.

WATER HIGHWAY
Kupreanof Island's natural beauty emerges as early morning fog begins to clear. Frederick Sound, seen in the background, surrounds part of the island. The sound is on the marine highway that enables ships to weave among the many islands of the Inside Passage.

established Fort St. Michael on the site where the town of Sitka now stands. The Tlingit rose up and destroyed the fort in 1802, but Baranov's contingent resettled Sitka in 1804. The Russians vanquished the Tlingit, built a town, slaughtered sea otters, and stayed until 1867. In that year, the United States, under President Andrew Johnson, purchased Alaska from Russia for the sum of $7.2 million.

At one end of town is Sitka National Historical Park, where an impressive collection of totem poles depicts Tlingit lore. At the other end stands St. Michael's Russian Orthodox Cathedral, its golden spires a contrast to the otherwise forgettable rooftops. A short walk to the top of nearby Cannon Hill yields a great panorama of the town.

Due east of Sitka lies Admiralty Island National Monument, home to one of the greatest concentrations of Alaska brown bears in the entire state. The brown bear is the same species as the grizzly—*Ursus arctos horribilis*—but lives primarily in coastal areas, eats more fish, and is larger. So many bears inhabit this island—an average of one per square mile—that the Tlingits once called it *Kootznoowoo*, or "Fortress of the Bears." Bald eagles have also found a haven here, building their huge nests—often more than 12 feet wide and 6 feet deep—in the old-growth spruce and hemlock forests along the shore. Approximately 90 percent of Admiralty Island lies within the national monument. The only permanent settlement, Angoon, is accessible by ferry or by daily flights from Juneau.

Southeastern Alaska has many towns and villages but only one city—the state capital of Juneau—located due north of Admiralty Island. With 30,000 residents, Juneau has a big-city feel about it. It also has warmth, history, a remarkable mountainous backdrop, and an attractive waterfront on Gastineau Channel. The Mendenhall Glacier reaches to the edge of the city. All summer long, helicopters and small planes carry sightseers over the glacier, sometimes even landing there, at other times climbing higher still to the Juneau Icefield in the Coast Mountains east of the city.

A RIVER OF ICE

The Juneau Icefield is one of three icefields in the Inside Passage, the others being the Stikine (near Petersburg) and the Brady (in Glacier Bay National Park and Preserve). Flying over any of them is a powerful experience, for the earth below suddenly ceases to be green and blue and becomes instead a vast sea of white ice—a vision of what much of North America looked like during the ice age 10,000 years ago. Glaciers flow from icefields much as rivers flow from lakes, albeit much more slowly. Snow typically falls every month of the year on an icefield, with each successive layer compressing those below it until the crystals actually melt and refreeze into dense ice, often thousands of feet thick.

Life is sparse on icefields and glaciers, but not absent. Iceworms—half-inch-long relatives of earthworms—live on the surface of the ice, where they eat algae, pollen, and spores. In turn, birds, such as snow buntings and water pipits, feed on the iceworms.

From Juneau, the journey moves yet farther north up Lynn Canal—one of the longest and deepest fjords in North America—to the towns of Haines and Skagway. With only 1,500 residents, Haines sits beneath the Chilkat Range and Cathedral Peaks with unassuming small-town

NATIONAL EMBLEM
The Inside Passage is one of the best places in North America to spot the bald eagle, which was designated the U.S. national emblem in 1782. Approximately 10,000 adult bald eagles live in this region.

charm. Founded in 1879 by S. Hall Young, a Presbyterian missionary and friend of John Muir, Haines today hosts the annual Southeast Alaska Fair for four days every August—a grand celebration filled with contests, music, and crafts. The largest gathering in Haines, however, is not of people but of birds. Every November to January up to 3,500 bald eagles converge on the nearby Chilkat River to feast on a late run of chum salmon.

GOLD-RUSH FEVER

Skagway marks the end of the line up the Inside Passage. (Those with automobiles can drive from either Haines or Skagway inland by highway to Canada's Yukon Territory and interior Alaska.) This vibrant town sits in the bottom of a deep mountain cleft, every ounce of its gold-rush history on proud display. And that's plenty because from 1897 to 1899 tens of thousands of stampeders trundled off steamers from Seattle and San Francisco to begin the arduous overland trek to the goldfields of the Klondike. The Porcupine Mining District, about 25 miles north of Haines, experienced its own gold rush during the same period; the area yielded several million dollars' worth of gold.

Today visitors to Skagway can savor the rambunctious history of gold-rush days as they stroll the wooden sidewalks past the false-fronted buildings

FAIR HARBOR

The town of Sitka boasts a spectacular natural setting, two colleges, and one of the largest collections of Tlingit and Haida Indian totem poles in the world.

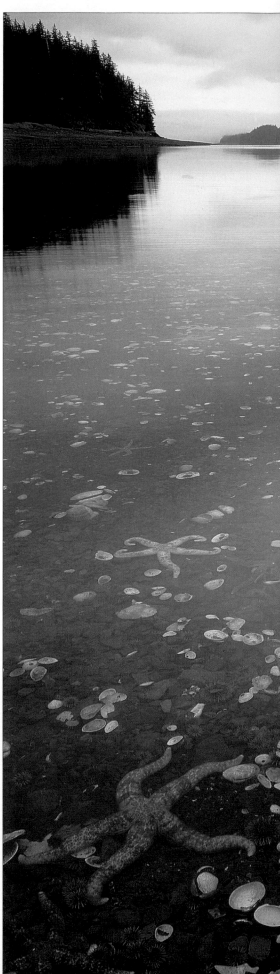

114

RUSSIAN HERITAGE
The octagonal St. Nicholas Russian Orthodox Church is one of the landmarks of Juneau. Completed in 1894, it is the oldest remaining Russian Orthodox church in south-eastern Alaska. Its interior is deco-rated with antique icons.

STARFISH CITY
At low tide the crystal-clear waters of Gambier Bay reveal a multitude of starfish and purple-blue mussels. The waters of the region are so rich in sea life that the Tlingit Indians have a saying: "When the tide is out, our table is set."

ELBOW ROOM
A lonely wooden cabin stands within the 16.8-million-acre Tongass National Forest—the nation's largest national forest.

JUNEAU'S GLACIER
Mendenhall Glacier, far right, is located just 15 miles north of Juneau. A visitor center on the shore of a nearby lake affords a dramatic view. For an even more spectacular look, the surefooted can hike the West Glacier Trail, which climbs 1,000 feet above the Mendenhall.

COOL CRADLE
A harbor seal and her newly born pup rest on an iceberg in Tracy Arm, below. Tracy Arm and Glacier Bay are Alaska's most prodigious seal-pupping areas.

of Broadway Street, poking into shops, and watching horse-drawn buggies clip-clop to and fro. No other place in southeastern Alaska puts on a show like Skagway. When the last ship leaves in the fall, the local people begin a welcome hibernation.

West over the Chilkat Range from Skagway and Haines is Glacier Bay, a landscape of mountains, inlets, islands, and forests that only a few centuries ago did not even exist. The 65-mile-long bay was buried beneath one massive glacier—in some places more than 10 miles wide and up to 5,000 feet thick. Captain George Vancouver charted the bay in 1794, noting that it was just five miles in length. When naturalist John Muir made his first of four visits in 1879, the glacier had retreated an astounding 30 miles up the bay and had split into two main tributaries. As the glaciers retreated, plants took hold and the newly uncovered land began to come alive. Both Vancouver and Muir noted the tremendous natural forces at work; the great rivers of ice ever

eroding, depositing, and sculpting the land. Visitors to Glacier Bay today can marvel at the power and majesty of these great ice sheets.

On his last visit to Glacier Bay as a distinguished member of the 1899 Harriman Alaska Expedition, Muir was able to behold further changes to the landscape visible to his own eyes since his first visit 20 years earlier. But it was Henry Gannett, a colleague of Muir's and chief geographer of the U. S. Geological Survey—the government mapping agency—who captured the vast magnificence of Glacier Bay and of the Inside Passage when he wrote: "For the one Yosemite of California, Alaska has hundreds." Then he added prophetically: "The Alaska coast is to become the show-place of the earth, and pilgrims, not only from the United States, but from far beyond the seas, will throng in endless procession to see it. Its grandeur is more valuable than the gold or the fish or the timber, for it will never be exhausted."

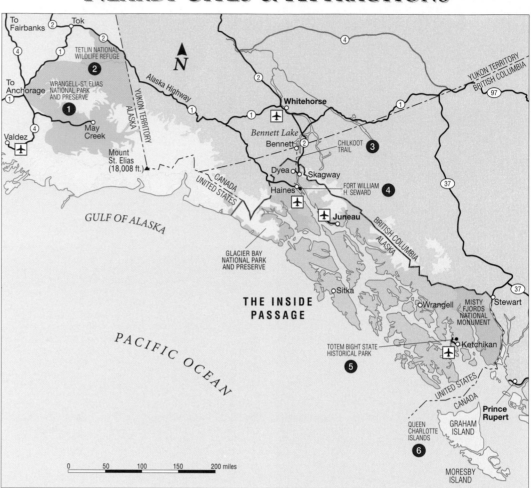

Totem Bight State Historical Park displays totem poles of the Haida and Tlingit Indians. Each of the carved and painted birds and animals on the poles figure within the legends and mythologies of these native peoples.

1 WRANGELL-ST. ELIAS NATIONAL PARK AND PRESERVE

This 13.2-million-acre park is the largest national park in the United States and a World Heritage Site. Four major mountain ranges—the Alaska, Wrangell, Chugach, and St. Elias—converge within the park's boundaries. These lofty peaks include nine of the highest summits in the nation; the tallest is Mount St. Elias, which at 18,008 feet is the third-highest peak in North America. Of the park's more than 150 gargantuan glaciers, Malaspina Glacier is larger than the state of Rhode Island. This wild and isolated landscape is home to Dall sheep, mountain goats, bison, black bears, and wolves. During the summer, wildflowers carpet the alpine slopes and the tundra supports a variety of plant life. Two unpaved roads run through a portion of the park and lead to the old gold and copper mining towns of Nabesna, McCarthy, and Kennicott. Located 200 miles east of Anchorage off Hwy. 4.

2 TETLIN NATIONAL WILDLIFE REFUGE

This is a region of great geographical diversity— 700,000 acres of rolling hills, thick forests, snow-capped mountains, and hundreds of lakes and ponds. Within the refuge the Chisana and Nabesna rivers merge to form the Tanana River. These rivers and lakes have burbot, grayling, and northern pike. Forests of birch, aspen, willow, and black and white spruce provide a habitat for black bears, grizzly bears, moose, coyotes, wolves, lynxes, and red foxes. Small fur-bearing animals, caribou, and Dall sheep are also found within the refuge. Spring thaw brings a host of waterfowl to the wetlands. The Pacific loon, osprey, bald eagle, trumpeter swan, three species of ptarmigan, and sandhill cranes are among the 150 species of birds that rest in the refuge during migration periods. Located 30 miles southeast of Tok on Hwy. 2.

3 CHILKOOT TRAIL

The 33-mile-long Chilkoot Trail runs from Dyea, Alaska, to Bennett, British Columbia. This physically demanding trail was blazed by thousands of prospectors who flocked to the goldfields of the Klondike in the 1890's. For three years fortune seekers struggled over these treacherous mountain passes, leaving relics of their journey scattered along the trail—rusty tin pots and pans, worn-out leather boots, and other objects. Hikers can trek a section of the trail, which is open only in the summer; the entire trail takes three to five days to complete. The route encompasses three different vegetation

zones: coastal rain forest supports western hemlock and Sitka spruce; the alpine tundra is treeless, dotted with the occasional shrub and low-growing willow; the dry subalpine zone is cloaked in lodgepole pines, alders, and alpine firs. Bald eagles, hoary marmots, mountain goats, river otters, and wolverines inhabit the region. As an alternative to the trail, the White Pass and Yukon Route Railroad offers excursions between Skagway and Bennett. The trail is located 9 miles north of Skagway.

4 FORT WILLIAM H. SEWARD

Named for the secretary of state who was responsible for the purchase of Alaska from Russia in 1867, the fort was established in 1898 to maintain law and order in the territory. The Alaska gold rush of 1898–1904 lured many hopeful prospectors to the region, forcing the government to take measures against increased lawlessness. The massive snow-capped peaks of the Chilkat Range form a spectacular natural backdrop to the fort's white buildings and its nine-acre parade ground. The fort saw active service until 1946, when it was incorporated into the town of Port Chilkoot as a historic site. Today some of the fort's buildings house artists' studios, which are open to the public. The Alaska Indian Arts workshop, located in what once served as the fort's hospital, provides demonstrations of some of the traditional crafts of the region, including the carving of totem poles and tribal masks. The Arts Center is home to the world-famous Chilkat Dancers who perform the traditional dances of the Northwest Coast Indians. Totem Village, a reconstructed Tlingit village, is also on the grounds of the fort. Located in the town of Haines.

5 TOTEM BIGHT STATE HISTORICAL PARK

Situated on a cove overlooking Tongass Narrows and surrounded by a stately coastal forest, this park contains 14 restored or replicated totem poles, as well as a reconstructed 19th-century Tlingit community clan house. A totem pole near the clan house displays traditional totem forms, all of which have symbolic meaning. (The eagle, for example, represents peace and friendship; the raven is a symbol of the Creator.) Visitors may tour the interior of the house, which contains a central fire pit used for

cooking and a wooden platform for sitting and sleeping. A pathway overlooking the Narrows leads to the other totem poles in the park, carved by both Haida and Tlingit Indians. Located 10 miles east of the town of Ketchikan.

6 QUEEN CHARLOTTE ISLANDS

Home to Haida Indians for more than 10,000 years, the 150 islands that make up the Queen Charlotte archipelago lie 55 miles off the mainland of British Columbia. Skidegate Channel separates the two main islands—Graham Island to the north and Moresby Island to the south. Graham Island contains the major communities, including the seaside towns of Queen Charlotte City and Skidegate, as well as the Delkatla Bird Sanctuary and Naikoon Provincial Park. Three-quarters of Moresby Island lie within the Gwaii Hanaas National Park Reserve. Anthony Island, at the tip of Moresby, contains one of the world's best collections of Haida totem poles. The islands are home to Sitka deer, beavers, racoons, and elks, as well as the hairy woodpecker and Steller's jay. Of the islands' 450 species of mosses and liverworts, five are found nowhere else on earth. Gray whales feed and calve in the offshore waters during their annual migration. Located 55 miles west of Prince Rupert, British Columbia.

Morrow Lake is one of the natural attractions along the Chilkoot Trail. The trail climbs above the tree line to an elevation of 3,680 feet.

At the foot of the Wrangell Mountains in Wrangell–St. Elias National Park, colorful McCarthy Lodge is a reminder of the pioneer heritage of this former mining town.

GAZETTEER: *Travelers' Guide to Great American Journeys*

Montezuma Pass in Coronado National Memorial, Arizona.

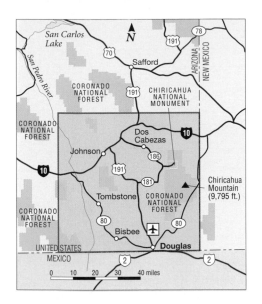

It takes a trip to southern Arizona's Cochise County—home of authentic cowboy saloons, untouched ghost towns, and rugged countryside—to fully grasp that the legendary westerners lived, gambled, and spilled real blood.

Tombstone, "the town too tough to die," was named by prospector Edward Schieffelin, who was told he would find "nothing else but his tombstone" in the Apache-dominated San Pedro Valley. The site proved to be rich in silver ore, and by 1881 the town was booming with gambling dens, dance halls, brothels, and saloons—the swankiest being the Crystal Palace Saloon, with its tin ceiling and mahogany bar. The Bird Cage Theater was named for its 14 birdcage compartments hanging from the ceiling, in which ladies of the night entertained their clients. Other highlights include Boothill Cemetery and the Tombstone Courthouse State Historic Park, where law officers tried to reign in rabble-rousers rougher than the wildest stallions. Tombstone's wooden buildings are free of the slick look of most revival towns. The O.K. Corral, a simple horse pen, sets the scene for reenactments of the most famous gunfight in history: the Earp-Clanton showdown of October 26, 1881.

Mining towns flourished and withered, but Bisbee was one town that didn't go bust. Gravity-defying houses perch on hilltops overlooking Brewery Gulch in the canyon below. The onetime bawdy district is still hopping, only now the Gulch's

Chiricahua National Monument contains many unusual geological formations created by volcanic activity in the area. A hiking trail leads to the Heart of Rocks region.

shops, eateries, and grand old Copper Queen Hotel are highly reputable. At the Queen Mine, visitors can don hard hats, slickers, and miners' lamps and travel into the shaft's murky depths.

Apache chief Cochise's abode in the Chiricahua Mountains was decorated with towering spires and strange rock pinnacles created by volcanic eruptions and erosion. Today quirky names identify the unusual geological formations: China Boy, Punch and Judy, and the Organ Pipe. Now encompassed by the Chiricahua National Monument, the area's sunny spots support yucca and cacti; Apache pine and Douglas fir cover the slopes. The vast Coronado National Forest surrounds the monument, offering prize trout fishing at Canyon Lake and good rock climbing on the eastern side of the forest.

BIRD-WATCHER'S PARADISE

But southeastern Arizona is more than a mecca for Wild West aficionados—it's also a bird-watcher's delight. A landscape of mesquite scrub, grassland, desert, and mountains supports an abundance of

birds. Visitors can spot gray hawks, vermilion flycatchers, and green kingfishers at the San Pedro Riparian Conservation Area and try to distinguish among Ramsey Canyon Preserve's 14 species of hummingbirds. The Willcox Playa is the winter roosting area for about 12,000 sandhill cranes, and the community hosts a celebration dedicated to sandhill cranes called "Wings Over Willcox" the third weekend in January.

The backcountry's palette of wildflowers and cactus-strewn desert valleys are dotted with ghost towns, such as Johnson, Dos Cabezas, and Paradise. In Gleeson, a hand-painted wooden sign reads "Pop. 21." Dusty roads and decrepit buildings whisper of a bygone era. With the rattling of an ancient saloon sign, modern-day visitors could swear they hear the dull thump of boot heels on the wooden sidewalk.

FOR MORE INFORMATION:
Cochise Visitors Center, 1500 North Circle I Rd., Willcox, AZ 85643; (602) 384-2772.

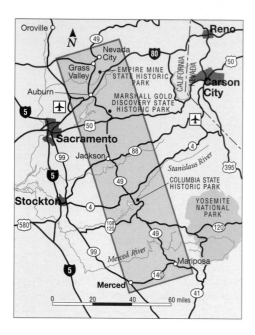

An old mining wheel in Jackson is a rusty reminder of the gold fever that led many prospectors to northeastern California in hopes of striking it rich.

In 1848 a massive source vein of auriferous quartz bursting with soft gold was discovered in northeastern California. Named the Mother Lode, the find gave birth to mines, boomtowns, and Hwy. 49—a road linking the settlements that quickly sprang into being as more than 800,000 fortune seekers swarmed into the region. Although the Mother Lode's bounty has dwindled, the Golden Chain Highway still yields precious nuggets of history and mining lore. From Mariposa to Nevada City, the highway winds through 267 miles of rugged canyons, lush valleys, and high plateaus of the Sierra Nevada.

The first cry of "Gold!" was uttered by James Marshall, who found three pea-sized chunks in the tailrace of a mill along the American River. A statue of Marshall points to the discovery site in the Marshall Gold Discovery State Historic Park. The site also encompasses Marshall's cabin, a Chinese general store, and a replica of the mill.

Auburn Ravine swarmed with prospectors bearing rusty pans after Frenchman Claude Chana hit paydirt in his first pan of gravel a few months after Marshall's find. First a temporary tent city, Auburn soon boasted brick and iron saloons and shops where customers paid for pork, cigars, and brandy with gold dust.

By 1860 the streambeds were panned out, and the region welcomed Cornishmen with deep-mining skills who settled in Grass Valley. Miners flocked to the valley to ogle Lola Montez as she skillfully shook wooden spiders out of her garments in her famous "Spider Dance." The Lola Montez House is dedicated to the eccentric dancer, who kept a bear on a chain in her front yard.

STRIKING IT RICH

Modern travelers can try their luck panning for the precious metal at the Deer Creek Mining Company in Nevada City. Formerly an upscale mining town, as evidenced by the elegant, three-story National Hotel and the Nevada Theater, Nevada City was frequented in its heyday by the likes of Mark Twain and Jack London.

Empire Mine State Historic Park sprawls above the oldest and most prosperous hardrock gold mine in California. From 1850 to 1956, the mine's 367 miles of tunnels yielded 5.8 million ounces of gold. Visitors can venture down the mine's main shaft, hike trails in the park's 700 acres of backcountry, or tour Empire Cottage. Bedecked with rose gardens and ornate fountains, this English manor house was owned by William Bourn, Jr., who operated the mine during its golden age.

Stagecoach rides, a working blacksmith, and shops run by costumed employees make the Columbia State Historic Park a living chronicle of gold-rush life. The town has barely changed since the 1850's, and its frontier-style buildings with upper-story porches and peaked roofs have appeared in many western movies.

Although the gold has long been panned out, Hwy. 49 contains one more precious treasure. Just outside of Mariposa stands the Giant Grizzly—a 2,700-year-old giant sequoia tree with a girth of 96.5 feet.

FOR MORE INFORMATION:

California Division of Tourism, 801 K St., Suite 1600, Sacramento, CA 95814; (800) TO-CALIF.

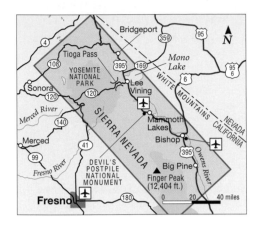

On the eastern slopes of the High Sierra, nature pulls jagged mountains, burbling hot springs, and peculiar rock formations from its bag of geological tricks. Running two-thirds of the length of the state of California, the Sierra Nevada is one of the longest mountain ranges in the world. The eastern slopes of the High Sierra are accessible to visitors via Hwy. 395, known as El Camino Sierra—the Sierra Highway. Completed in 1916, the Big Pine to Bridgeport section of the road spans wilderness regions that offer visitors opportunities for hiking, rock climbing, horseback riding, and fishing, as well as other outdoor activities.

One of the best ways to experience the serenity of this landscape of high deserts and verdant forests is on horseback. Many local pack stations offer trips ranging from hour-long horseback rides to customized, week-long hunting and fishing excursions. Some pack stations even invite visitors to help herd horses and mules from winter ranges in Owens Valley to their summer homes in the High Sierra.

Trotting through Tioga Pass, lucky riders may catch a fleeting glimpse of bighorn mountain sheep clambering nimbly over the rocky slopes. Just past the entrance to Yosemite National Park, the immense granite domes of Tuolumne Meadows offer spectacular views of the park's high country. In June, the meadow is carpeted with a profusion of wildflowers. Deer, squirrel, and coyote make their home in Yosemite Valley—a glacier-carved canyon where riders can stop for a swim in the Merced River.

The Mammoth Lakes region is a medley of craggy peaks, glacial lakes, and glistening streams. Mammoth Mountain's 30,000 vertical feet of ski runs make it the largest

The snowcapped spires of the Sierra Nevada rise to 14,000 feet, dominating the landscape of the Eastern Sierra region.

downhill ski resort in the nation. Some of the runs at Mammoth Mountain remain open as late as the Fourth of July.

A UNIQUE LANDSCAPE

The High Sierra region takes in several unusual geological formations created hundreds of thousands of years ago. The craters at Mono Basin National Scenic Area were formed by volcanic eruptions at the bottom of an inland sea. Mono Lake's alkaline waters mingle with underwater springs to create fantastic mineral formations known as tufas. In the middle of Inyo National Forest, the six-sided lava columns of Devil's Postpile National Monument stand some 60 feet in height. Formed 900,000 years ago, these impressive formations stand side by side like pipes in a giant organ. Nearby at Rainbow Falls, sparkling mists form prisms in the sunlight as the San Joaquin River cascades over the hardened lava ledges. The geological display continues at the bubbling thermal pools of Hot Creek Geologic Site, renowned for fly-fishing and choice catches of brown and rainbow trout.

Northeast of Bishop, a 4,600-year-old tree called Methuselah still clings to life

From its source in the High Sierra, near Yosemite National Park, the San Joaquin River tumbles through Sierra National Forest.

at Ancient Bristlecone Pine Forest. Their gnarled roots woven among the rocky ridges of the White Mountains, these wind-whipped ancient pines are the oldest documented living organisms, having sprouted their needles during the time of the pharaohs of ancient Egypt.

FOR MORE INFORMATION:

Mammoth Lakes Visitors Bureau, 3393 Main St., P.O. Box 48, Mammoth Lakes, CA 93546; (619) 934-2712 or (800) 367-6572.

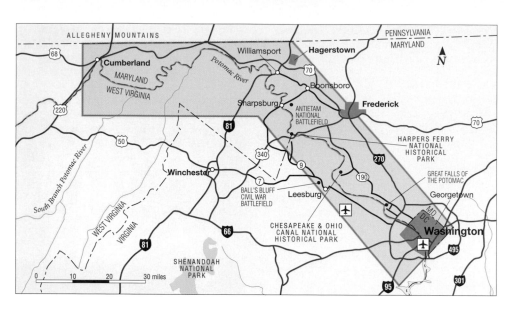

HISTORICAL HIGHLIGHTS

The region is steeped in history. Leesburg, chartered in 1757, features walking tours of its 19th-century historic district and the Ball's Bluff Civil War Battlefield. Harpers Ferry National Historical Park was the site of abolitionist John Brown's famous raid on the U.S. Armory in 1859. Near Sharpsburg, the Antietam National Battlefield preserves the site of the bloodiest battle of the Civil War. On September 17, 1862, Confederate general Robert E. Lee invaded Maryland with 40,000 troops and was defeated by an 85,000-man Union force; 23,000 men died in that single day of fighting.

The town of Cumberland was founded in 1749 as a trading post known as Will's Creek. It was the departure point for George Washington's expedition against the French in 1754. Cumberland's strategic location at the end of the canal transformed it into a hub of commerce for the Ohio Valley. Housed in a 1913 railroad station, the Cumberland Visitor Center displays photos and memorabilia relating to the canal and to the B&O Railroad.

FOR MORE INFORMATION:
Superintendent, C&O Canal National Historical Park, P.O. Box 4, Sharpsburg, MD 21782; (301) 739-4200.

The Chesapeake & Ohio Canal, more commonly known as the C&O, was born on July 4, 1828, when President John Quincy Adams lifted the first shovelful of dirt at the groundbreaking ceremonies. It then took 22 years for a legion of diggers, stonecutters, masons, carpenters, and black-smiths to build a waterway 184.5 miles long, 80 feet wide, and 7 feet deep between the tidewater at Georgetown and the pied-mont of the Allegheny Mountains in Cumberland, Maryland. The canal's 74 locks lifted or lowered boats along a 605-foot change in elevation. More than a dozen times a day, 87-foot-long canal boats towed by mules slipped through the locks to make the five-day journey between Georgetown and Cumberland alongside the mighty Potomac River.

Construction of the C&O was an engineering feat that transformed the lives of rural villagers living west of the Alleghenies. In 1800 the region had fewer than a million souls. Thirty years later it was booming with commerce, and its population had more than tripled.

The C&O was doomed to obsolescence even before it was completed. The tracks of the Baltimore & Ohio (B&O) Railroad, begun on the same day as the canal, reached Cumberland in 1842, eight years before the canal diggers. Canals could not compete with the speed and reliability of the rails. The flood of 1889 drove the canal company into bankruptcy; the flood of 1924 sealed the canal's fate.

Today all 184.5 miles of the canal are preserved within the Chesapeake & Ohio Canal National Historical Park. This oddly shaped park is only 60 feet wide in some places. Where the old oak-bottomed canal boats once drifted, canoeists, anglers, and ice skaters now enjoy the canal. The 12-foot-wide towpath, tramped by the mule teams of an earlier day, today hosts hikers, cyclists, and equestrians. Visitors enjoy picnics at Great Falls on the spectacular Potomac Rapids, canal boat rides, fishing rodeos, interpretive trails, and cultural events such as the C&O Canal Days Festival, celebrated in August in Williamsport.

A narrow canal boat glides along a placid stretch of the Chesapeake & Ohio Canal.

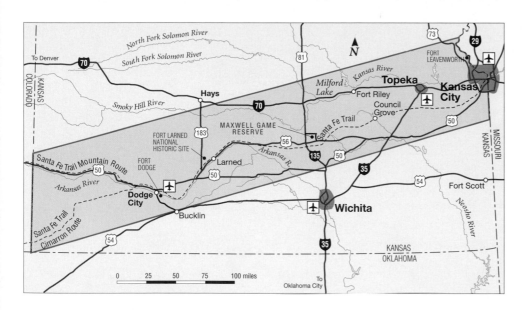

The Maxwell Game Reserve's buffalo herd is a reminder of the vanished lords of the grasslands.

In 1821 debt-ridden frontiersman William Becknell ventured into the prairies hoping to trade with the Indians, only to make his fortune in Santa Fe. Becknell's path was soon carved into a road by the caravans of covered wagons and mules, whose owners were driven westward by dreams of riches. Modern travelers retracing the route through this panoramic landscape, historic towns, and wildlife reserves will find the journey as compelling as the destination.

From Independence, Missouri, the 900-mile trail meanders through Kansas, Colorado, Oklahoma, and New Mexico, but almost two-thirds of the Santa Fe Trail stretches across Kansas. Far from deserted, these grasslands were home to the Pawnee, Osage, Kansa, Kiowa, and Cheyenne Indians, who stood little to gain from the trail. When blood began to spill along the vital trade link to New Mexico, military posts such as Fort Leavenworth, Fort Riley, Fort Scott, and Fort Larned sprang up to stanch the flow.

Established in 1859, Fort Larned acted as the Indian Bureau from 1861 to 1868 and was the site of negotiations with native tribes. Agreeing not to block traffic along the trail, the tribes received annuities of bacon, wheat flour, coffee, sugar, beef, and tobacco. Visitors can roam the fort's nine original stone and timber buildings, which have been carefully restored, as well as one reconstructed building. They can also explore the land outside the fort's quadrangle, where Indians camped in animal skin tepees every autumn.

In 1825 an agreement was made with the Osage under the leaves of an oak tree at Council Grove. The stump of the tree is still there, among 17 other historic sites.

Traffic along the Santa Fe Trail moved in covered wagons such as the one at right, seen at Fort Larned National Historic Site.

The town was once a main supplier of timber, and its former prosperity is reflected in the elaborate masonry of the Farmers and Drovers Bank, listed on the National Registry of Historic Places. A more modest building of native stone, the Kaw Mission State Historic Site was once a boarding house for Indian boys. Seth Hays House, run as a restaurant since 1857, was built by the town founder, Seth Hays, grandson of Daniel Boone and cousin of Kit Carson.

Council Grove lies in the Flint Hills, whose 5 million acres of grassland are considered to be among the world's most lush grazing lands. Carpeted with wildflowers and bluestem grasses, the gentle hills are dotted with deposits of limestone flint. The Flint Hills Overland Wagon Train offers city slickers the chance to experience the unique countryside firsthand. Weekend "pioneers" travel in covered wagons and trade modern luxuries for the pleasures of nights spent under the starry prairie sky.

BUFFALO COUNTRY

The vast grasslands were also the domain of the buffalo, and frontiersmen feasted on buffalo meat. Overzealous hunting decimated the herds, but at the Maxwell Game Reserve more than 200 buffalo still roam through a 2,500-acre refuge. More than 600,000 ducks and 40,000 geese frolic in the natural wetlands of the 19,000-acre Cheyenne Bottoms Game Refuge, which is home to 300 species of shorebirds.

Trail sites are well indicated on the highway, but to follow the authentic Santa Fe

Trail, travelers can ride along 11 miles of the original route in the vintage cars of a train that runs from Dodge City to Bucklin. West of Fort Dodge is a long stretch of defined wagon tracks that shows how the Santa Fe Trail marked the country's landscape as well as its imagination.

FOR MORE INFORMATION:
Santa Fe Trail Association, Santa Fe Trail Center, R.R. 3, Larned, KS 67550; (316) 285-2054.

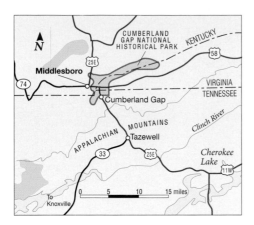

Pinnacle Overlook provides majestic views of the mist-shrouded rolling hills of the 20,000-acre Cumberland Gap National Historical Park.

Stretching from Maine to Georgia, the venerable Appalachian Mountains were once a formidable obstacle for Americans longing to settle the fertile lands beyond. But after Daniel Boone laid out a trail through the narrow Cumberland Gap in 1775, pioneers followed his lead, and by 1800 some 300,000 ambitious settlers had passed through the mountainous corridor to the west.

This entrance in the mountains was created when Cumberland Mountain was notched by Yellow Creek. Bison and deer trampled through the nick in the mountain to reach the pasturelands of Kentucky. Long before Daniel Boone, Indian hunters followed the migrating animals through the gap. The passageway was part of the Warrior's Path linking the Cherokees of the east with the Shawnee in the west.

Dr. Thomas Walker stumbled upon the Cumberland Gap in 1750, but American colonists couldn't take advantage of his discovery until the Treaty of Sycamore Shoals established peace with the Indians in 1775.

The Cumberland Gap and two miles of the original Wilderness Road are encompassed within the 20,000-acre Cumberland Gap National Historical Park—the largest national historical park in America. From Pinnacle Overlook, located near the town of Middlesboro, visitors are afforded an incredible view of the creek valleys and mountains of Kentucky, Tennessee, and Virginia, which converge at the Tri-State Marker, located in the park. A four-mile road leads to the 2,440-foot lookout.

The park is also crisscrossed with 50 miles of hiking trails. They range from short, self-guided nature trails to longer overnight hikes. Ridge Trail runs along the spine of Cumberland Mountain through 17 miles of forest and groves of mountain laurel and rhododendron. For an overnight stay on the trail, backpackers can rough it at four primitive campsites. Highlights of the trail include Skylight Cave, sunlit from a rock opening, and Sand Cave, whose cool sandy floor rises to a ceiling streaked with gold, red, and green earth tones. White Rocks, named for its white quartz pebbles embedded in sandstone, is located at the eastern end of Ridge Trail. From this vantage point, visitors can gaze over the rural countryside of Virginia and Tennessee.

One of the steepest and most challenging stretches of Ridge Trail takes visitors to Hensley Settlement, founded in 1904 by Sherman Hensley. This self-sufficient Appalachian community of 12 farmsteads flourished for almost five decades. Its inhabitants built their houses of hand-hewn chestnut logs and had a lifestyle similar to that of the pioneers.

CAVES AND FURNACES
Cudjo's (Soldier's) Cave was used as a hospital for Civil War soldiers, and it is said that the Society of Freemasons used to hold meetings within its chambers. The cave is also the site of the world's largest stalagmite, which rises 65 feet. The Newlee Iron Furnace, located near the village of Cumberland Gap, was built in the early 1820's. The 30-foot-high stack is made of large limestone blocks, which are delicately balanced to form a pyramidal shape. Visitors can walk under the casting arch of the furnace, where fiery molten metal once oozed out after it was fired.

Fort Lyon and Fort McCook attest to the Cumberland Gap's strategic importance during the Civil War. The South needed the gap to maintain vital east-west communications, while the North hoped to sever Confederate supply lines by capturing it, along with the East Tennessee and Virginia Railroad. The two crude earthwork forts changed hands four times, but the Cumberland Gap was never actually stormed. Of the Gibraltar of America, one soldier said, "It would have been murder to have ordered an assault."

FOR MORE INFORMATION:
Superintendent, Cumberland Gap National Historical Park, Box 1848, Middlesboro, KY 40965; (606) 248-2817.

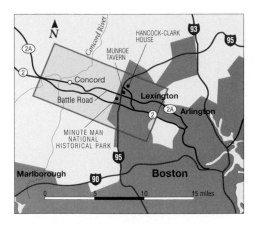

There is something about Battle Road as it winds through Minute Man National Historical Park that vividly evokes the opening of the Revolutionary War. Arching trees shelter a dirt-and-clay track used by horse-drawn carriages, stone walls mark verdant pastures, and wood-frame 18th-century structures—once homes or taverns—grace the roadside.

The history of Battle Road is celebrated in well-preserved houses, museum displays, statues, and plaques located at various spots along the way. Together they recount the running battle between 3,500 citizen militiamen and 1,700 British soldiers that took place between Lexington and Concord on April 19, 1775, imbuing previously ordinary sites—a small, rocky hill, a sharp bend, a rise, or a wooden bridge—with an unexpected significance.

To get a sense of how the day began for those 18th-century combatants, amateur historians can head over to Battle Green in Lexington at dawn. This is where Capt. John Parker mustered his 70-odd men to face 700 British soldiers. No one knows who fired the first shot, but within minutes, eight Yankee farmers were lying dead on the triangular patch of green. Their common grave is marked by a monument.

Nearby is Buckman Tavern, where many of Parker's men, alerted by Paul Revere's midnight alarm, anxiously waited until their final mustering at dawn. As Revere spread the news through town, he detoured to the Hancock-Clark House to warn John Hancock and Samuel Adams, who were spending the night there. Located just north of the green, the house contains exhibits relating to the battles, including the drum that 10-year-old William Diamond beat to summon the colonial militia to the green.

Munroe Tavern, at the east end of town, still looks much as it did that afternoon when it served as a command post for Lord Percy, whose 1,000-strong reinforcements had marched to the aid of the beleaguered British column. While the wounded were being tended, an American named John Raymond was pressed into service as a bartender. He was shot a few minutes later trying to escape out the back door. More than 5,000 men were involved in the fighting that occurred along the road between here and Menotomy (Arlington), and more men were lost that afternoon than in any other fight along Battle Road.

MESSENGERS ON THE MOVE

Troops were not the only ones on the move. Three patriot messengers—Paul Revere, William Dawes, and Dr. Samuel Prescott—rode through the countryside spreading the word of the British advance. At around 1:00 A.M. they were stopped by a British patrol; Revere was captured, Dawes turned back to Lexington, and Prescott evaded the British and made it to Concord and beyond. A boulder near the park's visitor center marks the site of Revere's capture.

North Bridge, a wooden replica built in 1956, spans the Concord River in Minute Man National Historical Park. The Minute Man statue, located near the bridge, was executed by Daniel Chester French.

An old stone wall dotted with crocuses marks a section of Battle Road. The Hartwell Tavern is visible in the background.

At the western end of Battle Road in Concord a commemorative bridge, which is a replica of the original, spans the Concord River. It was here that the Redcoats and Minute Men first exchanged fire. The Americans, mistaking the smoke rising from the burning supplies as a sign that their homes were being burned, confronted a detachment of British soldiers guarding North Bridge. In the shooting that followed, two Americans and two British were killed outright, and half the British officers were wounded. The British fell back and soon after began their retreat to Boston. North Bridge is flanked to the west by Daniel Chester French's Minute Man statue and to the east by a granite memorial obelisk that was erected in 1836.

FOR MORE INFORMATION:
Minute Man National Historical Park, 174 Liberty St., Concord, MA 01742; (508) 369-6993.

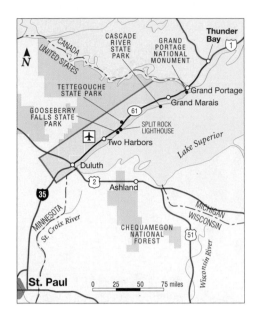

Cascade Falls tumbles through the rocky, forested splendor of Cascade River State Park.

Lake Superior is a fickle giant. Its mood can swing in a few hours from a placid inland sea to a churning froth of towering waves. For the traveler who chooses to meander along the craggy North Shore Drive (U.S. Hwy. 61), Lake Superior's ever-changing waters provide a seductive counterpoint to Minnesota's forested wilderness. This 150-mile route from Duluth to Grand Portage snakes along the shoreline, providing visitors with a closeup view of the lake.

Flanked on one side by the glacier-worn Sawtooth Mountains, the road passes through a land blessed with birch, quaking aspen, pine, and spruce, which are home to white-tailed deer, wolves, and moose. Here

and there the dense forest is slashed by rivers that rush pell-mell toward Superior, their powerful courses altered sporadically by glorious, bone-shaking waterfalls.

Capricious at the best of times, the lake is downright treacherous in stormy weather. To protect shipping, Split Rock Lighthouse was built in 1910. When completed, Split Rock's beacon could be seen for 22 miles. The restored lighthouse still looms 160 feet above the water's edge. The site includes a row of keepers' houses on the bluff near the tower, a brick light tower and fog-signal building, and a history center with exhibits on navigation, shipwrecks, and commercial fishing on the lake.

Despite the lake's temper, on a sweet summer's day it's easy to see why visitors take to the water in canoes, fishing boats, and kayaks. Between Gooseberry Falls State Park and Tettegouche State Park, a 20-mile stretch of shoreline called the Lake Superior Water Trail is being developed by the state of Minnesota. Following a coastal landscape of overhanging cliffs and stone arches shaped by the relentless power of water, paddlers enjoy the temporary quiescence of the giant at rest.

If venturing onto Lake Superior seems a trifle ambitious, visitors can seek out any one of the 2,100 wilderness lakes and 80

rivers and streams that grace the region. At Tettegouche State Park, there are four lakes to choose from, each stocked with walleye, northern pike, and brown trout.

FOREST AND LAKE

On a clear day, a hike up the 1,200-foot Lookout Mountain in Cascade River State Park, between Tettegouche and Grand Portage, yields a bird's-eye view of the region's eternal alliance between forest and lake: on one side, the endless unfolding of green forest, and on the other, the limitless blue expanse of Lake Superior.

Farther along North Shore Drive, near the Canadian border, the recently opened Grand Portage State Park includes a turbulent stretch of the Pigeon River and the Grand Falls, a thundering 130-foot cascade of foaming white water. Two hundred years ago, fur traders had to lug their heavily laden canoes through the rocky woods to get around the falls—hence the name Grand Portage, or "great carrying place." Near the head of the trail is Grand Portage National Monument, a reconstructed 18th-century fort and trading post that guarded the interior trade route on Pigeon River.

FOR MORE INFORMATION:
Duluth Convention and Visitors Bureau, Endion Station, 100 Lake Place Dr., Duluth, MN 55802; (800) 4-DULUTH.

Palisades Cliff, in Tettegouche State Park, overlooks Lake Superior at the northeastern end of the Lake Superior Water Trail.

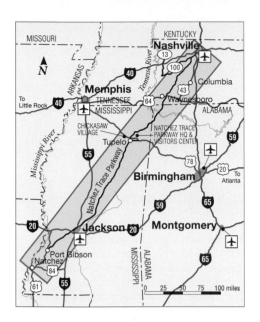

F or nature lovers, driving along the Natchez Trace Parkway's 450 miles of woods, rolling meadows, and bright fields dotted with cotton is sheer heaven. But this historic road, which wanders from Natchez, Mississippi, to Nashville, Tennessee, is more than just a billboard-free highway; it's a thread unraveling the story of Native American villages, Civil War battles, and the Old South.

When the United States acquired the Mississippi Territory in 1798, a series of Indian footpaths was the only route north from Washington, capital of the new territory. Dubbed the Natchez Trace, the trail became a thoroughfare for communication and trade after it was declared a postal route in 1800 and expanded by Congress in 1806.

By 1810 the Natchez Trace provided a trade circuit used by thousands of boatmen called Kaintucks, who floated down the Mississippi on flatboats loaded with tobacco, iron, and meat. After selling their wares in New Orleans, the rowdy Kaintucks invariably stopped at Natchez Under-the-Hill's saloons, brothels, and gambling dens before heading home. Natchez Under-the-Hill is now a cheery spot with a great view of the Mississippi, and its roisterous past only adds spice to the riverboat landing's charming shops and restaurants.

ARISTOCRATIC ARCHITECTURE

The town of Natchez, poised high above the Mississippi, was home to more than half of America's millionaires before the Civil War. The opulent mansions and lush gardens of the antebellum aristocracy present a dizzying display of wealth. Wearing frilled hoop skirts, guides from the Natchez Pilgrimage Garden Club lead visitors through stunning houses showcasing the massive columns and extravagant plasterwork of the Greek Revival style. The town's jewel may be Longwood, an ornate mansion with a pale blue onion dome topping America's largest octagonal house.

Just east of town, the reconstructed Grand Village of the Natchez encompasses restored sacred mounds and a museum describing the culture and way of life of the sun-worshiping Natchez Indians. The tribe's nobility were required to marry commoners—an arrangement that contributed to the stability of Natchez society.

On the way to Port Gibson, a segment of the Sunken Trace offers a fascinating hike among ancient trees whose gnarled roots protrude from the deeply grooved earth of the original trail. Port Gibson itself has elegant houses and churches pronounced "too beautiful to burn" by Ulysses S. Grant during his Vicksburg campaign.

At the Chickasaw Village stop, a nature walk reveals how the Chickasaw used native plants for food and healing, and an audio post describes the history of the people considered among the most fearsome warriors of Native America. Chickasaw chief George Colbert was a good businessman, too: he reputably charged Andrew Jackson $75,000 to ferry his troops across the Tennessee River in 1815.

Alabama's short section of the trace is laced with streams and burbling creeks; in Tennessee, branches of elm and black walnut arch over the roadway. Near Waynesboro, a 70-foot-long natural bridge was formed when a stream eroded a cave into the rock below. When the cave roof collapsed, a bridge was created, with one span reaching 50 feet above the streambed and a second only a few feet shorter.

In Tennessee, the town of Columbia features the home of President James K. Polk and a Greek Revival mansion called Rattle and Snap, named for a gambling match in which Polk's father won 5,000 acres of land from the governor of North Carolina.

FOR MORE INFORMATION:
Superintendent, Natchez Trace Parkway, R.R. 1, NT-143, Tupelo, MS 38801; (601) 680-4025 or (800) 305-7417.

Magnolia Hall, in Natchez, is a fine example of the wealth of antebellum architecture to be found at the southern terminus of the trace.

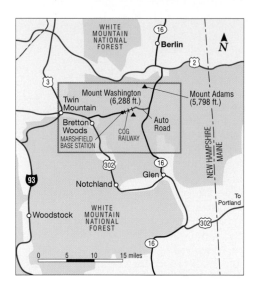

The traveler who observed that "getting there is half the fun" could have had the Mount Washington Cog Railway in mind. For more than a century, the steam-powered railroad has shuttled passengers to the top of New Hampshire's highest mountain, a 3¼-mile trip of mesmerizing sights—not the least of which is the train itself. An unlikely looking combination of a single passenger car, a coal tender, and a locomotive with a balloon-shaped smokestack, the train ascends the mountain on a track that averages a 25 percent grade. At Jacob's Ladder, a curving 300-foot-long trestlework, the train tilts to a dizzying 37.4 percent slope. The track is so steep at this point that a passenger in the front of the car is actually 14 feet higher than someone in the rear.

MARSH'S MACHINE
In the mid-1800's, many dismissed the idea of the mountain-climbing railroad as a mere figment of the imagination of local inventor Sylvester Marsh. But Crazy Marsh, as his detractors dubbed him, proved them all wrong with his design. The railway features a cog wheel that meshes with a rack in the center of the line, enabling the train to ratchet its way up and down the mountain at a stately four miles per hour. To compensate for the steepness of the track, the engine's boiler is angled so that it will stay level for most of the run. In 1976 the railroad was designated a National Historical Landmark.

The inaugural trip took place on July 3, 1869, with Old Peppersass—the original

As the Mount Washington Cog Railway puffs its way up the mountain, passengers are rewarded with a breathtaking vista.

"little engine that could"—hauling its first load of passengers. The railroad proved an immediate sensation, inspiring a reporter from *The Atlantic Monthly* to enthuse, "The horizon extends and admiration gives way to awe . . . . We drink in the wonder."

The journey has scarcely changed since those early days. In fact, some of the engines still in use date back to the 1870's. Passengers embark at Marshfield Base Station, tucked away in a valley of hardwoods and evergreens on the western edge of the mountain. With a blast of smoke and a few high-pitched toots, the train begins its journey. After stopping at the top of Coldspring Hill to take on a thousand gallons of water to cool the engine, the train resumes its progress toward the 6,288-foot summit. In the three-hour round-trip, the locomotive will burn a ton of coal.

ABOVE THE TREE LINE
Clearing the tree line—the elevation above which trees do not grow—the train emerges in a stark land of lichen-covered rocks, where only the hardiest plants, mosses, and shrubs can survive. This is, after all, the mountain where the highest wind on the planet—231 miles per hour—was recorded on April 12, 1934. Even in summer, temperatures can plummet below freezing, and winds exceed hurricane force more than 100 days a year. The mountain boasts 63 species of arctic plants, three of which— eyebright, mountain avens, and alpine cinquefoil—are found nowhere else.

The unparalleled view from the top offers a panorama of New England, encompassing six states. The other mountains of the Presidential Range—Madison, Jefferson, and Adams—cluster almost reverentially around their taller neighbor, a majestic testament to Robert Frost's claim that New Hampshire mountains seem to "curl up in a coil." On the far horizon lie Canada and the Atlantic Ocean. It is small wonder that P. T. Barnum called the view—and the trip—"the second-greatest show on Earth."

The mountaintop has been a popular vacation spot since the mid-19th century, when two hotels, the Tip Top House and the Summit House, opened for business. Today the fourth Summit House—built in 1980 on the site of its predecessors—offers refreshments and a brief repose for passengers before they board the train for the trip back to the valley below.

After a blast of steam and a couple of mournful toots, the train begins its descent. On the way down, there is plenty of time to reflect on the words of Pres. Ulysses S. Grant, who gazed out from this same cog railway in 1869 and observed, "Man seems so small when you look at the universe."

FOR MORE INFORMATION:
The Mount Washington Cog Railway, Rte. 302, Bretton Woods, Mount Washington, NH 03589; (603) 846-5404.

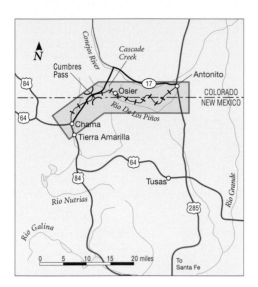

Outside Osier—the halfway point of the C&TSR route—the train crosses the 137-foot-high Cascade Creek Trestle.

At the historic railway yards in Chama, New Mexico, an engineer waits for the signal to take his train into the San Juan Mountains.

High in the southern Rockies, zigzagging back and forth across the Colorado-New Mexico border, the trains of the Cumbres & Toltec Scenic Railroad (C&TSR) travel a 64-mile ribbon of steel, preserving a part of the nation's railroading history and affording visitors an unforgettable feast of high-country scenery and unspoiled mountainous terrain.

This railroad—the longest and highest narrow-gauge railroad in the nation—runs between the towns of Antonito, Colorado, and Chama, New Mexico, crossing the state line no less than 11 times. Originally a spur line of the Denver & Rio Grande Railroad, the C&TSR was built in 1880 to serve the booming mining camps of the San Juan Mountains. Today it boasts a world-famous collection of original antique equipment and facilities, including six operating steam locomotives and more than 125 narrow-gauge passenger and freight cars.

Leaving Antonito in the morning, the train heads southwest into the San Juans through a landscape sprinkled with sagebrush. About an hour into the trip, the sagebrush gives way to tall ponderosa pines and groves of aspen as the train climbs west toward the valley of the Rio de los Piños, Spanish for "river of the pines." Passing through the first of two tunnels on the trip, the train reaches Phantom Curve, where many years ago a passenger train was struck by a snowslide and carried down into the canyon below. After passing through the second tunnel, passengers are rewarded with the most spectacular portion of the trip—Toltec Gorge.

Emerging from the 350-foot-long tunnel, the view of the Rio de los Piños—some 660 feet below—is nothing short of spectacular. Here the train's open-topped observation car is the best place to be. A few miles

farther is Osier, Colorado, where passengers disembark for lunch. At this point, the train from Chama arrives with its own load of passengers. Each day, the C&TSR runs a train from each terminal to Osier. After lunch, the trains return to their respective starting points. Passengers can purchase a round-trip ticket from either Chama or Antonito that will take them to Osier and back. Passengers who wish to see the entire line can take a straight-through trip, changing trains at Osier and returning by bus.

VIEW FROM THE TOP
On the way back to Chama, the train climbs to the top of Cumbres Pass before beginning the steep descent to the end of the line. Dense forest gives way to high mountain

meadows as the train pulls to a stop at the summit—an elevation of 10,015 feet.

After a pause for the locomotive to take on water and for the engineers to check the brakes, the precariously steep descent into Chama follows the valley of Wolf Creek for most of the remainder of the trip. Shortly after leaving Cumbres Pass, Windy Point provides a spectacular view down the valley.

In the late afternoon, the train rolls into the railroad yards in Chama—one of the best-preserved yards in the nation. Many of the structures, including the old repair shop, coal tipple, sand house, water tank, and depot, date from the turn of the century. The bunkhouse, built in the 1880's from hand-hewn local timber, provided overnight accommodation for train crews. It's best to tour the yards before the rail journey, because returning passengers immediately board the bus for the 50-mile road trip back to Antonito.

FOR MORE INFORMATION:
Cumbres & Toltec Scenic Railroad, P.O. Box 789, Chama, NM 87520; (505) 756-2151.

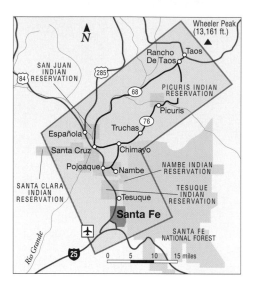

ew Mexico's High Road may not be the quickest route to Taos, but with time to spare and an appetite for Hispanic and Indian history, it is the best way to go. This 77-mile scenic route takes visitors along a series of small highways, following what Native Americans called the High Road. The route runs through a breathtaking landscape of pine, juniper, cedar, and silver sage; across valleys, rolling hills, and mountain ridges. In this tranquil backwater, where Spanish is still the dominant language, the small Hispanic villages look much as they did when they were settled more than 200 years ago.

Pueblo Indian history runs even deeper along the High Road. In the Española area, just north of Santa Fe, Pueblo Indian culture reached its zenith. The town of Española is renowned for its locally grown chili peppers. Today, in the pueblo villages of the Rio Grande Valley, Tewa Indians maintain a lifestyle that dates back more than a thousand years. The inhabitants of Tesuque, for example, have retained many of their political and spiritual traditions. In Pojoaque a few mounds are all that remain of the old pueblo, but a cultural revival has continued since 1973, when the Indians danced in their first public ceremony in more than a century. At Nambe Pueblo, visitors can see the remains of a kiva, once used for religious ceremonies.

Not far from these pueblos is the town of Santa Cruz, where the huge Church of Santa Cruz de la Canada, built in 1730, symbolizes the spirit of the first Spanish settlers. The town was once more important than Santa Fe, but is now a sleepy little place. There is little sign that Santa Cruz was once the focus of the Pueblo Revolt of 1680, the 1837 Chimayo Rebellion, and the 1847 Taos Revolt.

A few miles east along Hwy. 76, Chimayo is a picturesque farming village famous for its traditional weaving, distinguished by boldly colored stripes. Chimayo's church, El Santuario, is known as the Lourdes of the Southwest. In the sacristy is a *posito*— a little dirt well of sacred earth—which, according to the local legend, was used by Indians for healing. Healed pilgrims have left behind their crutches and braces in another room.

Chimayo's lovely, twin-belfried adobe church is set among cottonwood trees. The chapel was built in the 1800's by a local man who miraculously recovered from an illness on this spot.

MOUNTAIN SPLENDOR

The natural scenery along the High Road is spectacular. Located 8,600 feet above sea level, the town of Truchas offers stunning views of the Truchas and Trampas peaks, the Rio Grande, and—on clear days—even of La Plata Mountains of Colorado. Amid the stunning scenery and cool mountain lakes of the Pecos Wilderness Area sits the town of Picuris, the smallest and most isolated of the Indian pueblos. A museum recounts the roots of the earliest inhabitants of this area, which date back to A.D. 900.

Before beginning the descent to Taos, U.S. Hill offers visitors a magnificent perspective on this historic landscape. Mystical Taos Peak towers above the green valleys, while Wheeler Peak, New Mexico's highest point, pierces the clouds at 13,161 feet. Here, under the brilliance of a limitless sky, the High Road's blend of Indian and Hispanic culture is an unforgettable journey back in time.

FOR MORE INFORMATION:
New Mexico Tourism Department, 491 Old Santa Fe Trail, Santa Fe, NM 87503; (505) 827-7400.

For centuries farmers along New Mexico's High Road have cultivated melons, squash, and corn. These crops were the staple foods of the Pueblo Indians and their ancestors, the Anasazi.

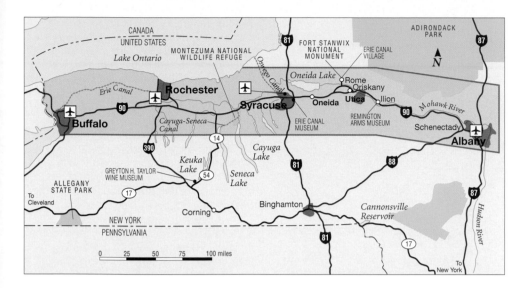

It's hard to imagine New York State without Buffalo, Rochester, Syracuse, Utica, or Albany, but the cities that spurred America's Industrial Revolution practically owe their existence to the Erie Canal. Completed in 1825, this 340-mile waterway runs between the Hudson River and Lake Erie. Constructed without the aid of a professional engineer, the canal included 18 aqueducts and 83 locks. The Erie Canal opened up the only trade route west of the Appalachian Mountains and played a key role in westward expansion. Whether hiking, motoring, cycling, or boating along this historic passage, visitors will discover that each set of the canal's locks unseals another fragment of its past.

At a cost of $7 million, the Erie Canal was, in its time, the most ambitious state-funded project in American history. The investment soon paid off as industry mushroomed along the canal. Reminders of the early development of the region include the Remington Arms Museum in Ilion, which displays prize weapons made by the famous Remington Arms Company. In Oneida, stainless steel flatware was just one of the numerous business ventures of the Oneida-based Bible Perfectionists, a religious group active from 1848 to 1880. In Rochester, photographic pioneer George Eastman's Georgian mansion houses the renowned International Center for Photography.

After railways supplanted canal transport, traffic on the Erie Canal declined. In the 1980's the canal was revived as a recreational waterway. Today just a few pleasure boats and the odd barge ripple the Erie's placid waters, now part of a 524-mile inland waterway network called the New York State Canal System, which also takes in the Oswego, Cayuga-Seneca, and Champlain canals. The Erie Canal gently flows past apple orchards, meanders through small towns, and links together miles of elegant canal-side homes. Farmland gives way to forests of sugar and red maple, black willow, quaking aspen, sycamore, and Scotch pine. Sometimes a white-tailed deer emerges to drink from the canal's edge.

Boaters can soak in the scenery from their own vessel or rent a craft from one of the numerous marinas. The Erie's 34 locks are kept in working order by second- and third-generation lockkeepers, who often pause to chat while helping skippers "lock through." Landlubbers can hike or bike along the Canalway Trail.

A LIVING MUSEUM
Rides on mule-drawn packet boats are available at the 1840's Erie Canal Village in Rome, located close to where the ground was first broken for the historic waterway. Authentic buildings were moved from within a 50-mile radius to create the period town, including a blacksmith shop, a train station, and a schoolhouse. Syracuse's Erie Canal Museum displays a wealth of canal artifacts in the 1850 Weighlock Building, a one-of-a-kind structure formerly used for weighing canal boats.

History goes back even further at the Fort Stanwix National Monument, where the original Stars and Stripes was raised for the first time in 1777. Now faithfully reconstructed, the fort was successfully defended by 550 Americans against 1,400 British soldiers. The Oriskany Battlefield, just west of the town of Oriskany, is the site of one of the bloodiest battles of the American Revolution. The site includes a visitor center and self-guided trails.

THE FINGER LAKES
South of the canal lie the Finger Lakes, linked by the Cayuga–Seneca Canal. According to Indian legend, the lakes were formed when the Great Spirit pressed his hand into the earth. The leisurely pace of life here hasn't changed since settlers took over the area from the Six Nations of the Iroquois in the 18th century. Country roads wind past quiet towns, and vineyards thrive in the temperate climate along the shores of the lakes. Wine lovers can sample vintages at wineries or visit the Greyton H. Taylor Wine Museum's collection of antique wine-making equipment. In the 6,400-acre Montezuma National Wildlife Refuge, great blue herons and 300 other bird species are protected amid flowering marshlands.

FOR MORE INFORMATION:
New York Canal Corporation, P.O. Box 189, Albany, NY 12201-0189; (800) 4-CANAL-4.

Visitors to Erie Canal Village, near Rome, can enjoy a ride aboard the horse-drawn canal boat Chief Engineer of Rome.

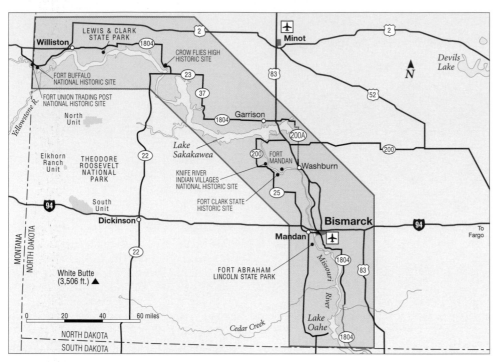

A reconstruction of Fort Mandan stands in a riverside park near Washburn. A snow-laden boat seemingly awaits the return of spring.

In early November 1804 a ragtag group of 40-odd men landed their dugouts and a 55-foot-long keelboat on the banks of the Missouri River near present-day Washburn, North Dakota. Morning frosts warned of the coming winter. Since May the explorers, under the leadership of Meriwether Lewis and William Clark, had toiled steadily 1,600 miles up the Missouri River. Ahead of them still lay the bulk of their arduous journey through uncharted territory to the Pacific Coast and back. But for now, under the watchful eye of neighboring Mandan Indians, the men paused for winter. Felling the tall cottonwoods that lined the river, they constructed a three-sided log fort and called it Fort Mandan.

The fort is one of 30 interpretive sites and displays along the historic Lewis & Clark Trail in North Dakota. Hwy. 1804 follows the east bank of the Missouri, and Hwy. 1806 travels along its western bank, allowing visitors to retrace Lewis and Clark's voyage of discovery in 1804 and their return trip from the Pacific in 1806.

Despite the damming of the river at Garrison that produced Lake Sakakawea—now ringed with numerous state parks and resort areas—much of the scenery along the route would still be familiar to those early explorers: rolling plains off to the east and north of the river, with the broken valleys, cliffs, and buttes of North Dakota's badlands to the west and south.

It was at Fort Mandan that Lewis and Clark met a pregnant 18-year-old Shoshone woman named Sakakawea, who acted as

an interpreter for the remainder of their journey. With her newborn baby strapped to her back, Sakakawea lent a disarming aura of domesticity to the expedition. Knife River Indian Villages National Historic Site offers a glimpse of what life must have been like for the peaceful Mandan, Kidatsa, and Arikara tribes of the region. Large circular depressions mark the locations of the Indians' earth lodges.

Elsewhere along the Missouri River, Lewis and Clark noted several other Mandan earth lodge settlements, including what is now the Fort Clark State Historic Site, a former fur-trading post. At On-A-Slant Indian Village, which derives its name from the Mandans' custom of building their villages on sloping hillsides, some of the reconstructed earth lodges are open to the public. The village is located within Fort Abraham Lincoln State Park, the site of George Armstrong Custer's last cavalry post. Visitors can tour the reconstructed Custer home, blockhouses, and other infantry buildings. A museum displays exhibits relating to the Lewis and Clark expedition, the Mandan Indians, and the military settlement.

During the expedition's return trip, Meriwether Lewis was accidentally shot by his one-eyed navigator, Cruzatte, who mistook him for an elk. An interpretive sign in the Lewis and Clark State Park, on the northern bank of Lake Sakakawea, recounts the incident.

FUR-TRADING POSTS

After Lewis and Clark's expedition, fur-trading traffic along the Missouri River increased significantly. Fort Union Trading Post was established in 1829, and it flourished for the next 38 years as buffalo hides replaced beaver pelts as the principal source of commerce. The post, with its 20-foot-high palisades and two-story stone bastions, has been carefully reconstructed. The fortifications are surrounded by the grassy plain where the Assiniboine, the Sioux, and the Crow once gathered to trade furs for goods shipped upriver by steamboat. Every summer, Fort Union Trading Post celebrates its past by hosting a re-creation of the day-to-day life of the fort, complete with costumed interpreters in period clothing.

FOR MORE INFORMATION:

Lewis & Clark National Historic Trail, National Park Service, 700 Rayovac Dr., Suite 100, Madison WI 53711; (608) 264-5610.

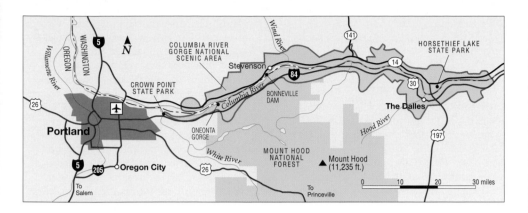

C arved through layers of volcanic ash and lava by ice age floodwaters, the 70-mile-long Columbia River Gorge is the only east-west break in the Cascade Mountains in the Northwest. Through it rushes the mighty Columbia River on its way to the Pacific Ocean.

To drive along the Columbia River Gorge is to witness a wilderness drama unfold: salmon battle upstream and cascades crash down the cliffsides. On the Oregon side, Hwy. 84 alternates with fragments of the Historic Columbia River Highway, "a poem in stone," engineered by Samuel Lancaster and completed in 1922. Based upon European models, the Columbia River Highway was designed to match, if not surpass, the beauty of Germany's Rhine River highway. Adorned with stone viaducts and bridges, the road follows the land's natural contours and leads to some of the gorge's best lookouts, such as Crown Point, a 725-foot-high bluff that offers a 30-mile vista of the Columbia River.

Beacon Rock, another lookout, was named by Lewis and Clark during their 1804-06 expedition: the volcanic remnant signaled obstruction-free river travel for the remaining 150 miles to the Pacific Ocean. Lewis and Clark were selected by Thomas Jefferson to log the geology and wildlife of this uncharted land and to attempt to forge friendly relations with the local Indians, who had lived in the region for more than 10,000 years. Pictographs and petroglyphs on the basalt cliffs at Horsethief Lake State Park are the traces left behind by these early inhabitants.

The gorge's distinct ecosystems range from sea-level vegetation to subalpine environments. At Oneonta Gorge, a narrow footpath winds past petrified trees, wildflowers, lichens, and mosses—many species of which are unique to the area. Biologists flock to the Columbia River Gorge to study endangered fauna, including the bald eagle and the arctic peregrine falcon, as well as endemic species, such as the larch mountain salamander.

WATERFALL PARADISE

The Columbia River Gorge has one of the world's greatest concentrations of waterfalls, including Bridal Veil Falls and Horsetail Falls—both named for their unique shapes. A rather fanciful local legend has it that Multnomah Falls, the river's highest waterfall, was named for a Multnomah chief's daughter, who hurled herself from the 620-foot precipice in the hope of saving the tribe and her dying lover from a deadly sickness.

Moving east toward the town of The Dalles, the green mountain scenery is abruptly replaced by a backdrop of semi-arid grasslands. The Dalles marked the end of a long haul for early pioneers roughing the Oregon Trail in the 1850's. At Bonneville Dam, a big paddle-wheeled steamboat makes a sweeping two-hour tour of the Columbia River. Fish aficionados can visit the Bonneville Fish Hatchery and watch salmon journey upstream from a glass-enclosed underwater visitor center. Anglers can hook sturgeon near Bonneville Dam, but Wind River, Hood River, and Klickitat River are the best places to catch river trout and salmon.

FOR MORE INFORMATION:

Friends of the Columbia Gorge, 319 SW Washington, Suite 301, Portland, OR 97204; (503) 241-3762.

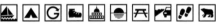

The Columbia River Gorge, right, is one of Oregon's most dramatic landscapes. The golden hues of autumn leaves, above, cloak the rocky ridges of the gorge.

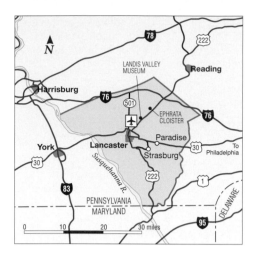

A visit to Pennsylvania's Lancaster County is a sojourn in a bygone era: this is the country of the Plain People—the Amish, the Mennonites, and the Brethren. These sects settled here in the early 1700's, welcomed by the Quaker William Penn's Holy Experiment of religious tolerance. Penn's experiment worked. Only 60 miles from Philadelphia, the Amish still maintain their convictions and their Old World traditions.

The simple Amish way of life lends the region an anachronistic charm: landscapes of small farms with neatly painted barns, windmills, apple orchards, and fields of corn and alfalfa. Local markets bulge with fragrant, home-baked breads, jams and jellies, relishes, homemade rootbeer, and colorful hand-stitched quilts. The sounds of Pennsylvania Dutch—a German dialect —can still be heard in small towns, such as Bird in Hand, where the Amish still wear traditional 19th-century clothing.

A HERITAGE PRESERVED

Early 18th-century Pennsylvania welcomed a wealth of immigrants, from Scottish Presbyterians, French Huguenots, and German Anabaptists to Welsh Quakers. Their talents in fine and decorative arts and technology made Lancaster the largest and most sophisticated inland community in America between 1760 and 1810. Lancaster County prospered from its iron foundries and water-powered mills, farming, and sophisticated furniture-making. During the Revolutionary War, the county was the granary and armory for the colonies, and for one brief day—September 27, 1777—the town of Lancaster (originally known as Gibson's Pasture) became the capital of the United States.

The Heritage Center of Lancaster County, in Lancaster City, is housed in the Old City Hall and Masonic Lodge on Penn Square. The center showcases the products of local artisans: fine Chippendale furniture, rifles, forged ironwork, and paraphernalia relating to the Conestoga wagon, a Lancaster County invention. From the late 1700's to the mid-1800's, horse-drawn covered wagons traveled along these rural roads and the 62-mile-long "turnpike" between Lancaster and Philadephia—the first long-distance, hard-surfaced highway in America, built between 1792 and 1794.

Today visitors can stroll through Lancaster's Old Town residential district of neat brick row houses. At the Landis Valley Museum, a re-created village of 18 historical buildings, artisans dressed in traditional Pennsylvania Dutch clothing showcase their talents. Lancaster's Central Market, with its distinctive Romanesque towers, was first established in 1730 as an open-air farmer's market. The Lancaster County Historical Society houses historical and genealogical archives, as well as local artifacts and memorabilia. Nearby, visitors can tour Wheatland—a restored Federal mansion built in 1828 that was home to President James Buchanan between 1848 and 1868. The Hans Herr House, built in 1719, is the oldest building in Lancaster City, as well as America's oldest Mennonite meeting house. Every autumn it hosts the Snitz Fest, a tasting of "antique" apples, from Sheepnose to Summer Rambo.

The Toy Train Museum in Strasburg displays hundreds of antique toy locomotives and cars. The Strasburg Railroad, America's oldest short-line railroad, takes passengers from Strasburg to Paradise in original 1851 wooden coaches, pulled along by coal-burning steam locomotives.

FOR MORE INFORMATION:
Pennsylvania Dutch Visitors Bureau, 501 Greenfield Rd., Lancaster, PA 17601; (717) 299-8901.

The Ephrata Cloister, a German monastic settlement founded in 1721, was one of America's first communal societies.

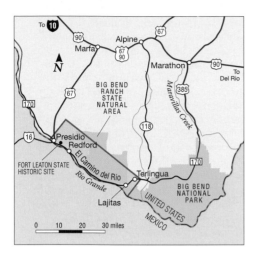

The desert environment of the Trans Pecos supports vegetation ranging from cacti to wildflowers. The proximity of the Rio Grande encourages the growth of nondesert species.

The Trans Pecos area of southwestern Texas is a land of stark and lonely beauty—granite and limestone mountains and jagged volcanic outcroppings; high desert slopes and flatlands strewn with bunchgrass, creosote, cacti, and wildflowers. This corner of the state, nestled against Mexico's northern desert, is home to mountain lions, mule deer, turkey vultures, and feral swine, as well as ghost towns, abandoned mines, and the ruins of forts and Spanish missions. It also is home to what has been described as the most scenic drive in Texas, and perhaps in the nation. Just as appropriately, the 50-mile stretch of El Camino del Rio (the River Road) along the Rio Grande between Lajitas and Presidio could be described as a drive from nowhere to nowhere else, but it is a satisfying sample of the region.

Lajitas (pop. 48) sits on the banks of the Rio Grande just west of Big Bend National Park. The town drew its name from the flat rocks (*lajitas* is Spanish for "flagstones") that line the riverbed here and once provided an easy crossing for Mexican bandits, Comanche raiding parties, gunrunners, and liquor smugglers. The town began, in fact, as an army outpost assigned to protect the territory from the infamous Mexican bandit Pancho Villa.

Today Lajitas is a recreational center for adventurers and fugitives from the rat race. Outfitters provide Rio Grande float trips and the Museum and Desert Garden holds a record of the rich history—from the Indians to the Spanish explorers to the quicksilver miners—that was written in the lonesome Chihuahuan Desert.

Driving upriver, Hwy. 170 hugs the Rio Grande for a few miles and then loops

north into the southern end of Contrabando Canyon, a name suggestive of the gulch's role in frontier lore. Returning to the river, the road passes an occasional stone dwelling on the Texas side, while across the river, the Mexican countryside fans out like an infinite, empty moonscape.

The tint of the earth changes according to the sunlight and shadows and the angle of vision: chocolate in the early morning, blanched ash at midday, and blue-black at sunset, when dusk lies in bands of color across the mesas and jagged ridges. The water, too, changes color and texture: smooth and turquoise where it runs over flagstone, and brown and frothy where it

Desert ferns add a delicate decoration to the multihued rock formations of the region.

picks up a tributary or scrapes silt from a shale embankment. At sundown, families of javalenas come out to scavenge the hillsides for edible roots, and pronghorn graze in grassy areas beside the water.

The road rises and falls with the rugged mountains—turning, dipping, and climbing. Past Tapado Canyon, the landscape begins to lose its harsh edge and rolls more gently toward Redford, a small agricultural town whose original name, El Polvo, says much about the hardscrabble fact of farming here: it means "the dust."

TRADING POSTS

Ten miles farther west, the road passes Fort Leaton State Historic Site, a reconstructed adobe fort that was a Spanish settlement until 1848, when it was acquired by Ben Leaton, a settler who turned it into a trading post. Presidio (pop. 3,310) also began as a trading post named for Presidio del Norte, a Spanish military encampment established on the south bank of the Rio Grande. With its low adobe buildings and uncluttered streets, Presidio still has the look and feel of a languid Mexican village.

FOR MORE INFORMATION:

Texas Department of Transportation, Travel and Information Division, P.O. Box 5064, Austin, TX 78763-5064; (512) 483-3727 or (800) 452-9292.

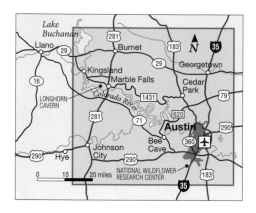

W inter in Texas is harsh only to the eye. The season drains the color from the northern prairies, denudes the oaks and maples in the central highlands, and stretches a drab and brittle skin over the endless farmlands and badlands of the west. But with the return of spring, a glow returns to the countryside once again. From March to October, the Lone Star State is splashed with some 5,000 varieties of wildflowers. Daisies, sunflowers, Indian paintbrushes, winecups, mountain pinks—blossoms of every color burst forth from the soil and make the land young again.

One wildflower in particular has inspired something close to a Texas religious ritual: the annual pilgrimage to the bluebonnet fields of the Hill Country north of San Antonio. To the Spanish, the flower was known as *el conejo* (the rabbit) because its white tip resembles a cottontail. Later, frontiersmen called it buffalo clover. Settlers, finding the flower similar in shape to a woman's prairie hat, gave it its present name. Though abundant throughout Texas (it is the official state flower), the most prolific bluebonnet growths are in central and southern Texas, from Austin to San Antonio, Corpus Christi, and Houston.

Bluebonnets begin to appear in March and are at their peak in mid-April. Small towns in central Texas celebrate their arrival with festivals of food, arts and crafts shows, music, group tours, and cycling excursions. Maps of marked trails—mostly networks of farm roads that run past the meadows where bluebonnets flourish— are published in newspapers. One of the most popular venues is the Highland Lakes Bluebonnet Trail south and east of Lake Buchanan, the sixth in a series of reservoirs that gradually rise 70 miles up the Colorado River from downtown Austin. This 41-mile triangular trail, with Burnet,

Kingsland, and Marble Falls at the points, circles through one of the most scenic patches of the Hill Country, which is widely considered the most picturesque region of Texas. Shaped by granite and limestone uplifts and by clear, spring-fed rivers, the hills support relatively little farming but sustain a rich array of natural flora—live oaks, junipers, cypress, and miles and miles of the beloved bluebonnet.

Lake Marble Falls is a popular destination for boaters, water-skiers, fishermen, campers, golfers, antique hunters, and rodeo buffs. Half a mile from the town of Marble Falls is Granite Mountain, an immense red-and-pink dome that was quarried during the 1880's to provide stone for the Texas state capitol in Austin. Since then stone from the quarry has been used in buildings throughout the world. The area's ancient geological formations serve up treasures to rockhounds. Nearby Longhorn Cavern—the third-largest cavern in the world—has been home to cavemen, Confederate gunpowder makers, and outlaws on the lam.

SPRING PAGEANT

North of the falls on Hwy. 281, the reason for the popularity of this trail becomes apparent as bluebonnets take over the landscape for their spring pageant. At Burnet the trail turns west onto Hwy. 29 and points toward Lake Buchanan, the largest of the six Highland Lakes. The lake's blue waters contain an abundance of striped and white bass, as well as catfish and crappie. Mesquite and cedar trees— home to bald eagles—dot the 124 miles of sandy beaches, mudflats, and limestone around Lake Buchanan's shoreline.

Past Buchanan Dam, the trail continues for a few miles toward Llano, then turns south to pass through Kingsland. All along the way, there are geological formations that are 600 million years old. But on a sunlit spring morning, when the fields are awash with the color of wildflowers, this land seems, indeed, as young as the season.

FOR MORE INFORMATION:
National Wildflower Research Center, 4801 La Cross Ave., Austin, TX 78739; (512) 292-4200.

A weathered barn provides a perfect counterpoint to a sea of blooming primroses and Indian paintbrushes, sprinkled with the region's beloved bluebonnets.

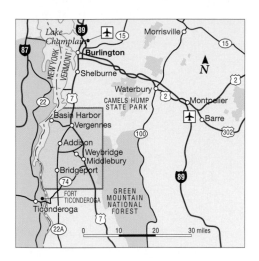

The lush Champlain Valley may have been designed with the Sunday cyclist and motorist in mind. A 51-mile circular route, leaving from the town of Middlebury and passing through Weybridge, Addison, Vergennes, and Bridgeport, provides a picture-perfect snapshot of Vermont's pastoral splendor. Nestled between the Green Mountains and the Adirondacks, these gently rolling back roads wind through white-steepled towns and over several covered bridges.

For drama, there is Lake Champlain. As the only New England state without a seacoast, Vermont must be content with the nation's largest body of fresh water outside the Great Lakes. And the 107-mile-long lake, which separates Vermont from New York and flows into Quebec's Missisquoi Bay, provides ample compensation. This region was once the sheep-farming capital of America, but the Champlain Valley also reveals a host of fascinating historic sites and even a treasure trove of naval history.

Middlebury, chartered in 1761, is the hub of Addison County's fertile Champlain Valley. This town is the perfect place to begin sampling the historic and scenic riches of the area. Its historic district, along Otter Creek, has nearly 300 buildings dating from the late 18th to the 19th centuries. Its white clapboard Congregational church, built in 1806, boasts an exceptionally well-built steeple that withstood the hurricanes of 1938 and 1950. The church's Ionic columns were each made from a single tree. The Sheldon Museum is the oldest incorporated community museum in the nation. The 1829 Federal-style house of Henry Sheldon provides a nostalgic peek into the daily life of 19th-century villagers. Visitors to the three-story brick mansion can tour the kitchen and parlors, as well as the Gallery and Research Center.

The verdant 1,200-acre campus of Middlebury College, established in 1800, has long attracted poets. Robert Frost taught here and helped to found the summer writer's conference. It's not difficult for travelers to imagine how this country of silvery aspens, beaver ponds, and fields of blueberries inspired the poet.

On the way to the postcard-perfect town of Weybridge, cyclists and motorists cross the oldest two-lane bridge in the nation. The three-spanned Pulp Mill covered bridge is one of only six such bridges still in existence.

When Abraham Lincoln hitched up his buggy, it was with a matched pair of Morgan horses, the small, sturdy, part-Arabian riding horse that is Vermont's state animal. Located in Weybridge, the Morgan Horse Farm, with some 85 registered Morgans, is a working farm dedicated to preserving this champion breed, whose

Vermont's many quaint covered bridges are among the Green Mountain State's most beloved landmarks.

lineage dates from 1790. The farm has a fine late-1800's barn covered with original slate roof tiles. Now a national historic site, the barn features a marble foundation.

MARITIME MEANDER
The picturesque town of Vergennes played an important role in the War of 1812. To counter a British naval attack from Canada, its shipyards constructed new boats of Vermont timber in record time, and the city's forges and furnaces worked overtime to produce 177 tons of cannonballs. These efforts enabled American forces to save Vermont from British occupation.

The Lake Champlain Maritime Museum at Basin Harbor documents the region's colorful maritime heritage. At the Battle of Valcour Bay in 1776, Col. Benedict Arnold's paltry fleet staved off a British advance. A replica of the 54-foot American gunboat *Philadelphia*, one of the vessels lost in the battle, is the museum's centerpiece.

After savoring the quiet beauty and historical highlights of this tiny section of Vermont, visitors return to Middlebury, where its village green beckons them to tarry awhile before heading home.

FOR MORE INFORMATION:
Addison County Chamber of Commerce, 2 Court St., Middlebury, VT 05753; (802) 388-7951.

Flanked by the foothills of the Adirondack Mountains, the Champlain Valley provides a quintessential snapshot of Vermont.

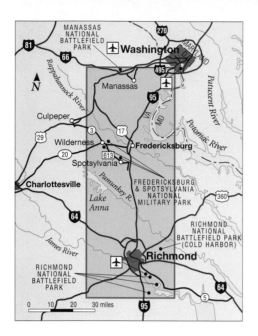

A memorial statue of Confederate hero Richard Rowland Kirkland is located within Fredericksburg and Spotsylvania National Military Park.

When brother fought against brother during the Civil War, Virginia's hills and meadows resounded with the sound of gunfire and the battlecries of opposing armies. Today a tour of battle sites, including Manassas National Battlefield Park, Fredericksburg and Spotsylvania National Military Park, and Richmond National Battlefield Park, allows history buffs to relive some of the most important clashes that took place in the state.

It was "the great skedaddle," as the headlong Union retreat from Manassas has been contemptuously dubbed. The day—July 21, 1861—had begun promisingly enough for the cocky, green volunteers as they fell on the equally green Rebels positioned along a gently flowing stream known as Bull Run, to the north and west of the town of Manassas. But by midafternoon it was clear that they could not sustain the speed required by their general's elaborate plan of attack. Timely reinforcements to the Confederate line following on the stubborn resistance of a previously untried Southern commander named Thomas Jackson—who stood like "a stone wall"—threw them back.

Thirteen months later, a second battle was fought in the rolling pastureland on the banks of Bull Run, and another defeat was endured by the Union Army, although this time the Northern cause was spared the humiliation of a rout. Both battles are commemorated at the 5,000-acre Manassas National Battlefield Park, located outside Washington on Hwy. 66.

The now-tranquil fields and woodlands look much as they did before the battles were fought. Self-guided tours, supple-mented by detailed maps and illustrations, enable visitors to follow the story of the warring armies.

A QUARTET OF BATTLES

Midway between the wartime capitals of Washington and Richmond, four battles were fought during the next two years in which more than 100,000 men lost their lives. The battlegrounds now lie within Fredericksburg and Spotsylvania National Military Park. Fredericksburg is remembered by many for the sheer pigheaded-ness of the Union commander, Gen. Ambrose Burnside, who, for hour after shattering hour on December 13, 1862, hurled his troops at the impregnable Confederate position behind a stone wall on Marye's Heights. Seven Federal divisions were butchered in the process. The next day a young Confederate sergeant, Richard Kirkland, repeatedly climbed the wall to take water to wounded Northern soldiers lying in the dirt. A statue was later raised to honor the Angel of Marye's Heights.

Twice Northern troops made it within sight of Richmond, the Confederate capital: the first time in 1862, when the two armies collided in what has come to be known as the Seven Days' Battles, and the second time in 1864, when Lee and Grant met at Fort Harrison and Cold Harbor.

At the Chimborazo Visitor Center in Richmond National Battlefield Park, visitors can obtain an overview of the defense of Richmond. Standing at Chickahominy Bluff, one can almost visualize Lee as he watched the early stages of the Seven Days' Battles. At Cold Harbor National Cemetery, gray stones stand in mute testimony to the 7,000 Federal soldiers slaughtered in an attack lasting less than 10 minutes.

FOR MORE INFORMATION:
Virginia Division of Tourism, 19th Floor, 901 East Byrd St., Richmond, VA 23219; (804) 786-2051.

The Stone House still stands within Manassas National Battlefield Park. The house served as a Union field hospital during the battles that took place here.

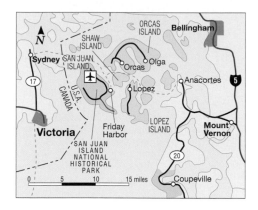

They have colorful names like Hat, Saddlebag, Samish, Guemes, Dot, and Huckleberry. Some of them have beaches, marinas, and museums. But most of the 172 San Juan Islands, scattered in the northern reaches of Puget Sound, are uninhabited—mere scraps of rock or floating carpets of thick fir trees draped with wild hanging mosses and sinewy madrono trees with blood-red trunks. Many of these islands are as pristine as they appeared to the 18th-century Spanish explorers who sailed here in their schooners and brigantines in search of the Northwest Passage.

Today island-hoppers cruising through this idyllic archipelago are rewarded with sightings of harbor seals, orcas, and minke whales, as well as spectacular views of the Cascade and Olympic Mountains. The four most developed islands—San Juan Island, Orcas, Lopez, and Shaw—are acces-sible via the Anacortes ferry, operated by Washington State Ferries, which departs regularly from Anacortes on the mainland.

THE PIG BATTLE

San Juan Island has a peculiar claim to fame. In 1846, a squabble over a pig turned the island into a political tinderbox that nearly exploded into a war between the United States and Great Britain. The Pig War—the stuff of a Gilbert and Sullivan opera—had its roots in the land dispute between the United States and Great Britain over the vast Oregon Country. The Oregon Treaty of 1846 gave the United States possession of the Pacific Northwest south of the 49th parallel, but neglected to specify who owned San Juan Island. Today relics of the military confrontation, in which the only casualty was the pig, are protected within the San Juan Island National Historical Park. The British Camp and the American Camp, located at opposite ends of the island, have restored garrisons, blockhouses, and officers' quarters. The Pig War Museum documents the story of this unusual battle.

On San Juan Island, hiking trails in Lime Kiln Point State Park wind under a canopy of ancient Douglas firs. Friday Harbor, the largest community in the islands, is home to the Whale Museum, which is devoted to the biology, natural history, and communication of these great sea mammals.

Orcas Island, the hilliest of the San Juans and largest of the four developed islands, has a thriving artists' colony. Orcas Island Pottery showcases some of the most highly regarded potters and ceramicists in the Pacific Northwest. The island also has more than 30 miles of hiking trails, some leading to the summit of 2,400-foot-high Mount Constitution. Orcas Island Historical Museum, housed in six log cabins, displays the work of island artists as well as Native American artifacts and relics of pioneer days. The Crow Valley School Museum re-creates a typical 1880's schoolhouse.

Lopez Island is ideal for cyclists. Its country roads meander past fields of grazing sheep and horses, and woods of pine and Douglas fir. Odlin County Park and Spencer Spit State Park boast sandy beaches and a protected lagoon. Shaw Island is the least-visited island on the Anacortes ferry route. But those who take the time to visit the island are charmed to find the Little Portion store and a small marina run by local Franciscan nuns.

FOR MORE INFORMATION:

San Juan Islands Visitors Information Service, P.O. Box 65, Lopez, WA 98261; (360) 468-3663.

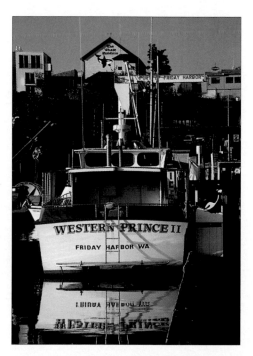

A cruise boat, above, awaits passengers at Friday Harbor, San Juan Island's main marina.

Shark Reef Recreation Site, left, is located on the windswept coast of Lopez Island.

INDEX

PICTURE CREDITS

Cover photograph by Jerry Jacka
2 Carr Clifton
5 Gary Braasch/Woodfin Camp
  & Associates

THE HUDSON RIVER

8, 9 Carr Clifton
10 (*upper left*) Carol Kitman
10 (*lower right*) Carr Clifton
12 Carr Clifton
12, 13 Ric Ergenbright
13 C.M. Glover
14 Timothy Eagan/Woodfin Camp
  & Associates
15 (*left*) Carol Kitman
15 (*right*) Carr Clifton
16 (*both*) Carr Clifton
17 Carr Clifton
18 Hancock Shaker Village, Pittsfield,
  Massachusetts
19 (*upper*) Gene Ahrens
19 (*lower*) Mike Yamashita/Woodfin Camp
  & Associates

THE BLUE RIDGE PARKWAY

20, 21 C.M. Glover
22 Frank S. Balthis
24 (*upper right*) Carr Clifton
24 (*lower left*) Alan Briere
25 Frank S. Balthis
26 (*left*) Carr Clifton
26 (*right*) John Elk III
27 (*upper*) Nenley-Savage/Stock Market
27 (*lower*) Erwin C. "Bud" Nielsen
28 Courtesy of the Virginia Department
  of Conservation and Recreation
29 (*upper*) Courtesy of the Richmond
  Convention and Visitors Bureau
29 (*lower*) C.M. Glover

THE OVERSEAS HIGHWAY

30, 31 James Kern
32 (*left*) Julie Robinson
32 (*right*) M. Timothy O'Keefe
34 Julie Robinson
34, 35 Bob Miller
35 Julie Robinson
36 (*upper*) Alan Briere
36 (*lower*) David Muench
37 (*left*) David Muench
37 (*right*) M. Timothy O'Keefe
38 M. Timothy O'Keefe

38, 39 M. Timothy O'Keefe
39 Timothy Eagan/Woodfin Camp
  & Associates
40 Jeff Foott
41 (*upper*) Bob Miller
41 (*lower*) Jan Butchofsky-Houser

MARK TWAIN'S RIVER

42, 43 Philip Gould
44 (*upper left*) Momatiuk/Eastcott/Woodfin
  Camp & Associates
44 (*lower right*) Jan Butchofsky-Houser
46 Philip Gould
46, 47 David Muench
47 Philip Gould
48 (*both*) Dave G. Houser
49 David Muench
50 Erwin C. "Bud" Nielsen
51 (*upper*) Courtesy of the Lauren Rogers
  Museum of Art
51 (*lower*) Philip Gould

THE OREGON TRAIL

52, 53 Geoffrey Clifford/Woodfin Camp
  & Associates
54 Ron Cronin
55 Dave G. Houser
56 (*both*) David Jensen
57 (*both*) Ron Cronin
58 David Muench
58, 59 Geoffrey Clifford/Woodfin Camp
  & Associates
59 Wolfgang Kaehler
60 Wolfgang Kaehler
61 (*upper right*) Daniel J. Dinges
61 (*lower left*) David Muench

RAFTING THE COLORADO RIVER

62, 63 Jeff Foott
64 Kim Heacox
65 Michael Collier
66, 67 Michael Collier
67 (*both*) Jeff Foott
68 Kim Heacox
68, 69 Carr Clifton
69 Glenn Randall
70 Jonathan Blair/Woodfin Camp
  & Associates
71 (*upper*) George H.H. Huey
71 (*lower*) Dick Durrance II/Woodfin Camp
  & Associates

DURANGO & SILVERTON NARROW GAUGE RAILROAD

72, 73 Kim Todd
74 (*upper left*) Kim Todd
74 (*lower right*) Bill Sciallo
76 (*upper*) Bill Sciallo
76 (*lower*) David Muench
76, 77 Kim Todd
77 Bill Sciallo
78, 79 Kim Todd
79 (*upper*) Frank S. Balthis
79 (*lower*) Randall K. Roberts
80 Randall K. Roberts
81 (*upper*) David Muench
81 (*lower*) George H.H. Huey

THE COAST STARLIGHT

82, 83 Frank S. Balthis
84 (*upper*) Bob Miller
84 (*lower*) Dave G. Houser
86 (*left*) Bob Miller
86 (*right*) Craig Aurness/Woodfin Camp
  & Associates
87 Frank S. Balthis
88 Catherine Karnow/Woodfin Camp
  & Associates
88, 89 David Muench
90 Jon Gnass
90, 91 David Muench
91 Jon Gnass
92 Bob Miller
93 (*upper*) Frank S. Balthis
93 (*lower*) Bob Miller

THE ROYAL ROUTE

94, 95 Al Harvey/The Slide Farm
96 Rita Ariyoshi
97 Rita Ariyoshi
98 David Muench
99 (*upper*) James Ariyoshi
99 (*lower*) Al Harvey
100 (*upper*) Al Harvey
100 (*lower*) Rita Ariyoshi
101 (*left*) James Ariyoshi
101 (*right*) Rita Ariyoshi
102, 103 (*all*) Rita Ariyoshi
104 Art Wolfe
105 (*both*) Buddy Mays/Travel Stock

THE INSIDE PASSAGE

106, 107 Carr Clifton
108 (*upper left*) Carr Clifton

108 (*lower right*) Erwin C. "Bud" Nielsen
110 Wolfgang Kaehler
110, 111 Carr Clifton
111 Jeff Foott
112 Tom Bean
112, 113 Carr Clifton
113 Wolfgang Kaehler
114 Carr Clifton
114, 115 Carr Clifton
115 Wolfgang Kaehler
116 Wolfgang Kaehler
116, 117 Carr Clifton
117 Wolfgang Kaehler
118 Wolfgang Kaehler
119 (*upper*) Tom Bean
119 (*lower*) Kim Heacox

GAZETEER

120 George H.H. Huey
121 George H.H. Huey
122 David Muench
123 (*upper*) Frank S. Balthis
123 (*lower*) David Muench
124 C.M. Glover
125 (*upper*) Jan Butchofsky-Houser
125 (*lower*) Bruce Hucko
126 David Muench
127 (*both*) Alan Briere
128 (*both*) G. Alan Nelson
129 James P. Rowan
130 Dave G. Houser
131 (*upper*) Tom Bean
131 (*lower*) Jan Butchofsky-Houser
132 (*both*) Dave G. Houser
133 James C. Simmons
134 David Muench
135 (*left*) Jeff Foott
135 (*right*) Gary Braasch/Woodfin Camp
  & Associates
136 Betty Crowell/Faraway Places
137 (*both*) Robert W. Parvin
138 David Muench
139 (*upper*) Dave G. Houser
139 (*lower*) Paul O. Boisvert
140 (*upper*) R. Anthony Todt
140 (*lower*) C.M. Glover
141 (*left*) Wolfgang Kaehler
141 (*right*) Rankin Harvey

Back cover photograph by Dave G. Houser

ACKNOWLEDGMENTS

Cartography: Map resource base courtesy of the USGS; shaded relief courtesy of the USGS and Michael Stockdale.

The editors would also like to thank the following: Lorraine Doré, Dominique Gagné, Pascale Hueber, and Cynthia Shannon.